Notes from

Pete Cross was born in Redruth in 1962 and grew up in Truro. He gained an honours degree from Bath Academy of Art, then spent the following fifteen years working in London publishing houses and travelling. On returning to Cornwall at the beginning of the new millennium, he began writing a column for *Cornwall Today*, which soon became known as *Backalong*. His children's book, *Shadows in the Sky*, was published in 2007 to widespread acclaim, and won the *Waterstones Holyer an Gof Special Prize*.

He lives in an old miner's cottage on the north Cornish coast with his wife, twin boys, and an assortment of chickens and geese.

Also by Pete Cross
Shadows in the Sky

Notes from a Cornish Shed

A choice selection of
Pete Cross' *Backalong* columns
from *Cornwall Today* magazine

ONE INCH

CAPACITY

First published in Great Britain in 2013 by
One Inch Capacity
www.oneinchcapacity.co.uk

ISBN 978-0-9926451-0-6

A catalogue record for this book is available from the British Library.

Jacket design by
in©

Jacket photography by Marek Paczynski Photography

Cornwall Today logo reproduced by kind permission of
Cornwall and Devon Media

Printed and bound in Cornwall by TJ International, Padstow

For Ern,

who didn't have to bugger off to Australia

Introduction

R ather fittingly, it was the return of the Cornish chough in 2001 that started all this.

Writing had never been a chore for me, and I was always jotting things down in my spare time. As a teenager I'd write daft, *Goodies*-inspired nonsense, then as an art student I produced earnest, terrible poetry. I'd also keep diaries and, when the mood took me, write the odd article. I didn't really try to get anything published until that amazing day when I went out on the cliffs at Predannack and saw those choughs flying over Cornwall for the first time. I'd only just returned here myself, and I couldn't believe three choughs had now joined me. The experience got me so choked-up that I just had to get something written down.

They published my rather emotional choughy piece in *The Times*, no less, and thus was launched a journey that I'm still on today. I started writing a regular piece in *Cornwall Today* magazine, and pretty soon the editor suggested I think up a name for my column. This took a bit of doing, largely because I couldn't easily sum up exactly what it was about. I'd originally considered writing it from the 'downsizing to live the rural dream' sort of angle. But that horse had already been flogged to within an inch of its life in magazine articles, newspaper columns, and books written by people with names like *Minty Fumble*, called things like, '*A Puffin on the Aga – How we left our six-figure salaries in London and bought a derelict lighthouse to live the dream in Cornwall with our many endearing pets, embarking upon numerous hilarious interactions with quirky but loveable locals'.* You know the kind of thing.

And besides, I grew up in Cornwall, so the place was already familiar to me. Not much novelty value there, because I was simply coming home. But what did strike me upon my return was how much Cornwall had altered from the place in which I'd grown up during the sixties and seventies. Not just the obvious things, like the fact that the little T-junction at Carland Cross was now a huge great roundabout. No, staring me in the face was the fact that Cornwall had caught on. The place I'd grown up in, this rural backwater, had become fashionable. Now this was interesting, and more than a little confusing. When I moved to London in 1985 I'd found myself suppressing my Cornish accent to try and fit in, and not be thought of as a yokel. But moving back to Cornwall in 2000, I found myself trying to recapture it, because being a proper local, with an accent to match, had become *cool*.

So I called the column *Backalong*, one of our nicer Cornish colloquialisms, meaning 'in the past'. At first I tended to focus on how Cornwall had changed. But as time went by I found myself writing about all sorts. I used the column as a unique opportunity to get an increasingly diverse range of subjects off my chest, from the quintessential smell of summer to why we should all learn to love gulls. People seemed to like it. I'm pleased to say the magazine has always given me delightfully free rein. If I had to describe the general theme, I suppose it would be something like, 'Cornishman returns after twenty years away, is amazed at how the place has changed, and concludes that it's still a great place to live'. Yep, I'd say that's about right.

This book, then, is a lightly edited selection of such columns from over the years. If you've already read them, I hope you've forgotten enough to enjoy them a second time. If they are new to you then I just hope they amuse/touch a nerve/make you think a little bit. I do get carried away at times, but I'm too much of a coward to want to offend anyone. That is unless you're a Jerusalem artichoke-loving, bottled water-quaffing, sanctimonious opera buff, in which case I don't honestly care. And if you're the sort of person who has an immaculately stacked pile of logs on display in your living room, but no intention of ever setting light to them, you might want to pop this back on the shelf and choose something else. I've heard Minty Fumble's very popular.

Anyway, a couple of last things: you'll find that the chapters are in no particular order. I'm not exactly telling a story here, so you can dip into it at any point, pick 'n' mix style. And the title: '*Notes from a Cornish Shed*'. Well, there's a shed in the back garden, and that's where I write. I'm guessing you'd probably got that.

Finally, and most importantly, I'd like to say thank you. If you're taking the time to read this now, or if you've read my column occasionally, or even regularly, over the past ten years or so, then I'm indebted to you. Writing *Backalong* is great fun.

Plus, it's saved me a fortune in therapy.

The good old days

2007

S o, as we Cornish emerge to reclaim our territory from the tourist hordes, blinking from the shadows like rudely awakened dormice, and reflecting on the season's worst excesses (the bathers who ignored the flags, the road rage incidents, the news stories about drunken teenage tombstoners…), and we say things like, "Thank goodness the crowds have gone!" and, "Well, at least the lanes aren't quite so jammed up now!" let us remind ourselves that our holiday season is actually not that bad.

It hit me the other day as I was browsing through my collection of old postcards of the village where I live. One recent acquisition was actually sent from here in 1949, and the scrawled message on the back is interesting. At the end of a lengthy diatribe about the weather, the holidaymaker has complained to her friend: 'It's getting spoiled like most places'. Which made me wonder, good grief, *how bad can it really have been back in 1949?* Had they put the price of deck chair hire up a farthing since 1948? Perhaps a beach hut had been erected where she'd liked to have parked her Austin 7. What exactly was she comparing it with?

Then I was reading T.O. Darke's charming little book, *The Cornish Chough*, published in 1971, in which he reminisces about '…a quieter time, before the aircraft came, and before the motor cars jammed the country lanes in summer'. What? 1971? Jammed? *Really*?

It must have been about the same year that I distinctly remember my Newquay hotelier Uncle Morley warning my parents to take care when they went out for the evening: "Newquay's getting some rough at night these days. Tin't like it was". Newquay, rough in 1971? Imagine what dear old Uncle Morley would be saying now.

The obvious conclusion is that it's simply in our nature to whinge. Always has been. I should know; I've done a fair bit of it myself. It seems to me that whatever period of history a particular person's life slots into, that person will spend a large proportion of it complaining that it isn't as good as it could have been.

Things are surely not that bad these days. Although my memory personally doesn't go back much beyond the late sixties, I can think of several reasons why Cornish life wasn't that much better back then. For example, on the beach it was considered obligatory to have a tinny transistor radio (to be replaced by the ghastly ghetto blaster in the eighties) installed in the lee of your windbreak. The noughties iPod revolution might be driving people mad on the horribly intimate London Underground, but on a Cornish beach the use of earphones has spelt the end of a particularly intrusive form of noise pollution. I have three overwhelming memories of the early seventies on the beach: getting changed in a huge towelling tube which had an elasticated hole for your neck, always going home with

11

black, tarry oil from the Torrey Canyon between your toes, and feeling violated by Simon Bates' cheesy 'Our Tune' on the radio everywhere you went. I'd only describe one of those three things as a force for good.

There was plenty of antisocial behaviour back then too. I remember personally at the end of a day's work on the farm, us teenagers sitting on the teetering top of a fully laden trailer-load of hay bales, trundling along behind the tractor, going back to the farm. As the queue of tourists' cars grew ever longer behind us, we'd find it hilarious to use our forefingers to count every car, in full view of the increasingly frustrated drivers. If that's not antisocial behaviour, I don't know what is. You certainly wouldn't see such things happening today, although that's probably got more to do with Health and Safety issues and the fact that the trailer would be rammed by an irate driver, enraged at the violation of his human rights.

Reading up about what my local area was like a hundred or so years ago, I see that my local beach isn't actually any more crowded than it was in Victorian times. Apparently even back then there would have been a vast influx on an August bank holiday. Admittedly these days people wouldn't walk four miles to get here from Redruth, and they require a car park twice the size of the village to cater for them. But at least we have public toilets now.

It's all relative. Sometimes I think we're a bit like those nimbies who complain about developers building a new house across the road, but not stopping to wonder what the inhabitants of the old cottage next door must have been saying when their own house was built. There can only be one conclusion. Although sometimes it seems there are more tourists than ever, and their cars go faster, and are parked less discriminately, and people are generally ruder, we'll all just carry on. We have always, and *will* always, worry that everything's becoming damaged beyond repair.

We need to try and enjoy what's still good, because the one certain thing is that it will all have changed again in another ten years. It's an incredible thought, but our children will look back at life in the noughties as the good old days.

Roses

2006

I was chatting to a friend about a rhododendron I'd seen. "What colour is it?" he asked, enthusiastically. "Dark green, obviously," I replied cleverly. "Except for a tenth of the year when it has an impressive mass of pale mauve flowers." OK I was being pedantic, but it strikes me that we gardeners are generally obsessed not with what plants look like, but with what a certain bit of them looks like for a very brief time. Namely their reproductive organs.

Flowers are overrated, for two main reasons. Firstly, they stick around for such a limited period that planning a garden becomes a mathematical exercise in split second timing in order to ensure the different areas are always sufficiently colourful. And I was never any good at maths.

Secondly, flowers are to blame for the vast majority of gardening jobs you'd really rather not be doing. You spend the whole year pruning, deadheading and feeding. Even when you're sitting down relaxing on a hot day you still can't really relax because you'll always have a niggling feeling that in some distant, long-neglected corner there are flowers crying out for your attention (I'm convinced no gardener can ever attain a state of true relaxation in his garden without the aid of at least half a bottle of Chablis or similar, and it's all the fault of

14

flowers). All this unnecessary angst is caused by the gardener's desperate obligation to force everything to produce a few more colourful sex organs. Flowers I mean. Life's too short I tell you.

No plant sums up the futility of this mind-numbingly desperate search for floribundance better than that traditional British garden cliché, the rose (I know *English* sounds more appropriate than *British* for roses, but we are in Cornwall). A nondescript, shapeless plant when not in flower, the rose demands our constant attention. It's always ill, needs ridiculous amounts of food, exact pruning, and when it does actually flower you're praying you don't get more than a light breeze or your lawn will instantly be scattered with an unwanted confetti of petals.

A shower of rain transforms the plant into a hopelessly bedraggled mess. To make things worse, every time you try to go near it, you are seized in an agonising and bloody grip from which you are afraid to move, for fear its vile prickles will ensnare you further. There aren't many plants that leave you needing a blood transfusion after a bit of light pruning. And if one of its foul barbs penetrates anywhere near a knuckle, you've got an aching reminder of the incident for the next few days. What's more, roses are divided into about fifty confusing groups and sub-groups, which wouldn't necessarily matter, except that you've got to identify it accurately in order to prune it correctly. If you get it wrong, guess what? You don't get any flowers.

Yet bizarrely, this sad excuse for a plant has been Britain's favourite since, well, since before anyone can remember. And

15

so we've endured several centuries of rose gardens: dull voids of equally spaced skeletal frames that do nothing all year and then just produce flowers for a bit, and then look rubbish again. Correct me if I'm wrong, but there are quite a few plants out there that give a lot more, and ask a lot less in return.

I suppose it's a bit unfair of me to blame the rose entirely. They didn't ask to be displayed so unimaginatively. And occasionally you see roses that look great. That spectacular *banksiae 'Lutea'* rambling over an old wall at Trelissick, or dog roses growing in a hedgerow, or delicate little burnet roses peppering the coastal landscape in June have all, on occasion, made my day.

I've managed to remove just about all the knackered old roses that came with my garden when we moved in six years ago. Oh yes, I've committed rosacide many times, and I throw myself upon the mercy of the court. Hell, I've enjoyed it, ripping those gnarled, woody old roots out and replacing them with something lovely. I'd recommend it to anyone. In some ways it's odd behaviour, when you bear in mind I live in an old cottage that should, by rights, have a rose scrambling around the door. But I've made a point of growing a passion flower there instead. A preferable plant in every way. The only rose I've left standing is an old American Pillar rambler that sprawls naturally over the wall by the back gate. I don't do anything to it, and it doesn't mind. Its leaves are completely riddled with black spot, obviously, because it's a rose, but even this looks quite nice. Any rose with vaguely interesting-looking foliage is a bonus in my book.

16

I've heard it said that roses don't thrive in Cornwall because the ambient soil temperature here doesn't get low enough in winter for the poor dears to enjoy the much-needed dormant period considered vital for flower development. There you go, as if you needed it, another great reason to live in Cornwall: not too many roses.

OK I'll reluctantly admit they smell nice. Some of them.

Fashion

2004

I 'm a stranger to fashion. As anyone who knows me will confirm, my modest little brain is incapable of grasping the concept of wearing something which, by definition, will no longer be considered desirable in a year or so's time. It doesn't make any sense. I don't ever buy anything unless I can confidently expect to be still wearing it in ten years. Ideally twenty. Boring, yes. Tight fisted? Possibly. I simply don't care.

I don't even understand the basics of fashion. I can see how its victims want to look radical. Hence it was when flares were at their absolute lowest fashion ebb that super-trendy people began wearing them again. It looked outrageous for about five minutes. The same happened with those appalling golfing jumpers with the diamonds. One minute they're laughed at, the next, they're *de rigeur*. But what I don't get is why these things are still desirable when every idiot's wearing one. First it's all about looking different. Then it's all about looking the same.

But now I've seen it all. Now things have gone too far. The one piece of clothing that has always been the preserve of Eddie Grundy, Compo and James Herriot is, apparently, this year's 'must have'. The Wellington boot. Trendy New Yorkers are wearing them in the city, festooned in a diverse range of patterns and colours. Girls are wearing them with mini skirts. Companies are racing to churn them out (no doubt with their designer label discreetly displayed). Wellies are *the next big thing*. Of course we've seen the same happen with Doc Martens, and other such workmanlike items. I can understand the appeal of taking something utilitarian and poncifying it. It's sort of cute, and ironic. Perhaps there are even surrealist echoes here. I may be getting out of my depth, but maybe it's a sartorial answer to Dadaism. Just as Marcel Duchamp produced a picture of a pipe with the caption, 'This is not a pipe,' so might the urban wax jacket wearer proclaim: 'This is not a country jacket primarily designed to be windproof and to protect me from injury whilst clambering through hawthorn and bramble in pursuit of the rabbit I've just shot'. But wellies? No! There's a fundamental difference here, people.

Now, I can't deny that wellies have always been a muted fashion statement, in an acceptably rural sort of way. There are shapely posh ones with fancy buckles, and cheap-and-cheerful ones without. Farmers wear black, yachty types wear yellow (always disdainfully referred to by my friends and I whenever we were enjoying a pint outside the Pandora Inn as the 'yellow welly brigade'), and posh county types wear green (the 'green welly brigade'). But they've always had one basic, primary function: *to stop your feet getting wet*. Whatever would the Duke himself make of all this 21st century silliness? When he started the whole welly thing in 1815, he designed them as a practical riding boot. Because of his iconic status (defeating Napoleon being no mean feat) and the fact that people apparently liked

19

their funky, modern, 'low cut' style, they caught on in a big way. Over the years, the style was developed to become a practical, chunky, waterproof gumboot.

But there's a time and a place. Encase any part of your body in rubber and it's obviously going to be getting pretty sweaty in there after a while. But your feet! Anyone who's ever worn wellies on a warm day knows what I'm talking about. Ever spent time in them without any socks on? Your pinkies end up sloshing about in there. Wellies are for when you're spending time in a field, end of story. Stithians Show, yes. Royal Ascot, no. Yet again, it seems like a clear-cut case of the Emperor's new clothes. Or in this case, wellies.

What the fashion victims seem to have failed to grasp, again, is that if you are young and gorgeous, you'll look good in anything. If you're not, you won't. I seriously read the other day that 'Wellies are at their best with a tiny miniskirt and tanned legs'. Rubbish. Wellies are at their best with that pair of jeans you're too embarrassed to take to Oxfam, a liberal coating of something brown, and a spaniel snapping at their heels. That's a cool looking pair of wellies, right there. The stunning miniskirted model they use to prove their spurious claim about the miniskirt will obviously have such spectacularly shapely pins that she'd look just as good in a hairshirt and a pair of flippers. Probably nicer, actually, but I'd better not let any personal fetishes cloud the equation. Actually, looking on the bright side it's probably only a matter of time until a hairshirt/flipper combo is the season's must have.

Maybe this fashion thing's not so bad after all.

Light at the end of the tunnel

2003

U nless you've been living on the dark side of the moon for the past couple of years, I'm sure you're quite aware that choughs returned to Cornwall in 2001. Then last year they bred successfully for the first time in over fifty years.

So naturally at the beginning of this year there was much speculation about whether we dared hope that they might do so again. Sure enough, in February the wonderful news broke that our Cornish choughs were showing signs of nesting for the second year running on the Lizard. The RSPB again put the wheels in motion to ensure that the nest was fully protected from the foul activities of egg thieves. Like last year, a military-style exercise was planned, involving staff and volunteers keeping a 24-hour watch on the nest site.

An appeal went out for volunteers. 'Lovely,' I thought. I didn't mind selflessly spending the odd sunny spring day sitting on a comfy chair chatting to people, watching the beach and getting a tan. This was going to be great. I could do my bit for our choughs and score brownie points with my wife. Best of all, it would be a lot easier than spending a strenuous day doing some other worthy voluntary activity like yanking

21

bindweed out of a reed bed or something. Surely voluntary work didn't come much cushier.

But as I considered which days I'd be available for shifts I realised they were shorter of people to cover the night shifts than the day ones. Feeling guilty and in an overwhelming and out-of-character rush of altruism, I put my name down for some. 'I'll just dress warm,' I confidently told myself. 'It won't be the first time I've stayed up all night. I must have done it at least once when I was at college.'

So it's now mid-April, four in the morning. I'm standing on top of the cliffs at Southerly Point on the Lizard. It's blowing a gale and the rain's just started again, stinging more this time as I realise it's now mixed with a healthy dose of hailstones. Moving gingerly closer to the edge I look down. It's terrifying. I stumble a little as my boot glances a clump of thrift. I curse it, then feel strangely guilty as I look down at the offending plant, happily pointing its fifty-odd pink flowers at me like perky little pom poms. How could it be so happy? I marvel for a moment at the ability of the most beautiful plants to grow in the most inappropriate situations, oblivious to the elements. I stand and stare. Not long now.

My thoughts flit over every subject. As I look blankly out over the raging Atlantic I hear the ghostliest sound. The deep, low boom of a ship's foghorn. It sounds just like hydrophonic recordings of whales I've heard. I start to imagine a pod of colossal blue whales, somewhere out there in the black infinity. I can't see a thing. The ship could be two miles out or two hundred. I wonder what it must be like for them on the ship, *out there.* And then I think, wait a minute, the passengers are probably either asleep, or drinking beer, or indulging in some other pleasurable night-time activity. They might be all the way out there, but chances are they're a whole lot better off than me. And they're going somewhere. Now I feel worse.

The weather forecast predicted a big area of low pressure coming up from the south, and it's no comfort to realise that I'm probably the first person in mainland Britain to witness this particular squall. I can't imagine there's anyone else stupid enough to be up at this time of night staring south into the gloom, and there certainly isn't anyone else on mainland Britain any further south than me. With a shudder my mind snaps back to the job at hand. There's something freezing trickling down my neck. The rain's stronger now, and I'm really starting to shiver. I tell myself, 'Never mind, it'll soon be over'. I stare into the vortex.

Suddenly there's a bleep in my pocket. I reach for my walkie talkie and press the button.

"Hello mate. All quiet on the southern front. You?" says the voice.

"Fine. Glad you called though, I was just drifting off a bit. Mind wandering, you know."

"Foul weather eh? I bet our red-billed chums are dryer than we are. Fancy swapping round on the hour?"

"Sure. The tide's well up now. Over and out."

One of the other volunteers on duty tonight flicks his spotlight on for a quick scan of the cliffs from his end, and I do the same with mine. I notice the first glimmerings of dawn as details out to sea start to become visible. The end is indeed in sight. What a night. What a ghastly night. Wish I'd gone clearing reedbeds.

*

A week later and I'm back again. Same shift, different world. Tonight it's beautiful. With almost a full moon you can see way out to sea. I could read a book by it, if I wasn't being so vigilant of course. The occasional passing cloud adds a nice sense of drama. It is wonderful to be out here, truly wonderful. I want to tell everyone when I get home, but deep down I know that I could never get this feeling across to people. There are too many senses involved. "Here, sniff this piece of hottentot fig while I describe the Lizard under a full moon," I could say. "And imagine the sound of the Atlantic surging in and out of vast caves." But it wouldn't work.

Maybe it's the moonlight playing on my imagination, but tonight my thoughts are obsessive. All I can think about are the egg thieves. They are the sole reason we're standing on this cliff in the middle of the night. The sad fact is that there is a small number of people in this country who, rather than enjoying any more commonplace criminal pursuits, get their kicks from pursuing that most old-fashioned of Enid Blyton schoolboy occupations: pinching rare birds' eggs. Well, not even rare birds' eggs. More 'birds' eggs in a rare place'. The chough isn't exactly a rare bird; it's just incredibly rare in Cornwall. Of course our choughs, being a member of the crow family, aren't stupid. They like to nest in dark crannies within inaccessible caves, making any kind of access to them

24

extremely difficult. But just like last year, the RSPB aren't taking any chances. It would be a dedicated egg thief indeed who could gain access to our sacred ones. I start to imagine James Bond trying it. You know, when he swims to the villain's island lair underwater in full scuba gear. On arriving at the beach he takes off the wetsuit, to reveal his immaculately pressed white tuxedo and AK 47. Minutes later he's dealt with the guards and is dancing with the villain's beautiful girlfriend and speaking fluent Russian. Of course 007 has far better things to do than go nicking birds' eggs.

Whoosh! I'm snapped back from my imaginary world by a night flying gull, a big black-back. Riding the updraughts, it swoops right past me and out into the vast seascape. How can anyone hate these beautiful creatures? They've got so much more right to be here than we have. Way out over the sea I hear the bird scream out. I wonder what on earth there is out there that could hear it. Maybe it doesn't matter. Maybe he's just screaming anyway. Maybe it just feels good. He's probably working out some issues of his own. He disappears around the headland. Tonight, the only thing really spoiling my perfect night is that I'm wearing too much. Two shirts, two fleeces and a lined waterproof jacket, together with waterproof over-trousers. This was all just the ticket a week ago. But tonight, during the five minute walk from the car park, I worked up such a sweat under there that now, well, I'll spare you the details.

An hour, or maybe two or three go by, and it's now quite light. Our beloved birds make their first foray of the day.

25

Whenever I'm watching our choughs I get a lump in my throat. It's almost as if I'm witnessing an impossibility, as if I'm just out for a walk and spot a dodo, or the Beast of Bodmin, or a Tasmanian tiger. But this morning is particularly special, because the choughs have only just got up, and we've been keeping them safe all night, and we're the only ones in the world who can see them right now. It's intimate. Of course all the birds are really doing is foraging for food. For them every day is life and death. But I, sentimental as ever, like to think they're saying, "Thanks pard".

Finally my replacement arrives and we swap round. I'm free to go. But unlike a week ago, this morning I'm in no hurry to leave. This morning this looks like the most beautiful place on earth, and I sit and take it all in. As ever when I'm up very early, I tell myself, 'I've really got to get up earlier in future. All this is on my doorstep every day, because I'm lucky enough to live here, and all I'm doing is sleeping'. But I probably won't.

An hour goes by and our birds do another tour. Actually it's just the male this time. The female is sitting tight. That's good. It's 9am now, and I'm getting horribly warm. Time to go. What a night. I wouldn't have missed it for the world. And to think, I could have gone clearing reedbeds.

Fitting in

2009

I was chatting recently to an incomer who had only just moved down here. "So how can I fit in with the locals then?" he was asking. "What's the best way to not stand out?" And do you know what the very first thing that came into my head was? No, you'll never guess. I found myself saying, quite spontaneously, "Just don't wear shorts in winter."

It's true though. This bizarre phenomenon, which I don't remember at all twenty or thirty years ago, appears to be on the increase, and it always seems to be incomers doing it. Oh, and, for some reason, postmen. And postwomen. Postpeople. It is surely the most obvious symptom of the 'incomer trying too hard to embrace some sort of self-perceived version of a Cornish lifestyle'.

Now, I'm not talking about that first sunny day in early April when we experience the novelty of spring sunshine on our skin, producing some strange chemical reaction, making us all panic and think, simultaneously, 'This could be it. Summer. I need to go out for the day in nothing but a pair of shorts and a T-shirt and take the roof down on the car and have lunch *al fresco* and then invite everyone round for a barbecue. Today'. We all know that twenty minutes later the wind will have got up, the sun a distant memory as it disappears for two months behind a haze of low-lying, thick Cornish mizzle, and we'll be freezing. But we've all done it. To do anything else just wouldn't be British. Similarly, I'm not talking about the dying days of an Indian summer, when it's mid-October, three weeks from Guy Fawkes Night, and there's still a bit of warmth in the air, and we judge our legs to still be adequately coloured to be presentable to the world, and we think, 'Oh, just one more day before I put the shorts away for the winter'.

No, I'm talking about the donning of shorts in January / February. The fact is that although polar bears may be noticing the tragic melting of their native habitat, that doesn't mean it's our duty to come out in sympathy by adopting summer leisurewear.

True, the average person moving down here from upcountry may have arrived somewhere that's warmer than where they lived before, but that doesn't make this Hawaii. You don't have to dress like this to prove that you've made the right decision to live here. It won't make the sun come out. And it doesn't look cool. Just cold.

It's not only young people doing it. It's a common sight to see retired couples soldiering through January, determinedly displaying their leathery legs of a deep ochre, often combined with an equally daft short-sleeved shirt. Admit it, you're in the UK. Mud Island. It's still relatively cold in winter, even in Cornwall. And even if it's a mild winter, then it's grey and drizzly all the time, so shorts look just as silly. This winter it hit minus 6.5° c. In my polytunnel. That very day, I saw a person in shorts. I rest my case.

Dressing skimpily isn't fooling anyone into thinking you've got some sort of maritime lifestyle. After all, people with a maritime lifestyle dress warm, on account of the fact that it is, more often than not, rather cold. You seldom see surfers, for example, dressing skimpily. Not the proper ones who go in the water, anyway. This is because they are always cold. For that reason, they tend to be in shoes, fleeces, hoodies, jeans, that sort of thing. They're not stupid.

Ah well. It's summer now, supposedly. So the danger of witnessing this uniquely British sartorial peculiarity is over for another year. Anyway I'd better shut up before I'm lynched by old people with goosepimply legs the colour of molasses. And hopefully my friend has taken heed.

Unless he's thinking of becoming a postman of course.

A heavy cross to bear

2003

Has anyone noticed what's happened to Kernow stickers lately? You know, those little black ovals with the white cross people stick on the boot of their car. It's all very strange. I've been getting my knickers in a bit of a twist about it all.

First a bit of background. The Kernow sticker is, of course, a version of our great flag. It seems there's no proven origin for the white cross on a black background motif, though the most popular explanation is the folk story about St Piran spotting molten tin among the burning black ore in his hearth. It took the shape of a cross, and he thus discovered the smelting process. Other explanations are many and varied. They include the flag being a version of the old Breton one, or the cross of St George with the colours changed. Or simply that it is a relatively modern invention, like the silly Devon one.

One thing's for sure. There's absolutely no escaping the ubiquitous flag of St Piran these days. Its popularity and exposure have gone through the roof with the recent surge of Cornish nationalism and general self-awareness. This is all fine by me, not that it matters. I'm not quite sure who first came up with the idea of sticking St Piran's motif on the back of their car, or when. But it's been around as far back as I can remember, and certainly a fact of life ever since I was growing up in the sixties and seventies.

Back then the Kernow sticker was rather like a membership card to an exclusive little club. The idea was to send out a subtle message. If your car was not originally registered in Cornwall, and therefore not blessed with the hallowed RL, AF, CV or GL on its number plate, then life wasn't really worth living for many Cornish people. You ran the embarrassing risk of being mistaken for someone from outside of our sacred land. Or even, I hardly dare say it, *a tourist*. The Kernow sticker provided a very neat solution. An easy escape from the appalling stigma of being seen driving around Cornwall in a motor that didn't belong here. It sends shivers up my spine what people must have gone through before it was invented. Let's face it, when we see another vehicle on the road, especially if it's misbehaving, we look at it for incriminating signs. We look at the model, the condition, the driver, and we make assumptions. Huge, sweeping generalisations. More importantly to us down here, we've always looked at the number plate. The most damning evidence of all. Spotting the 'out of county' number plate immediately issues us Cornish with a handy, 'Well, what d'you expect, they're on holiday!' sort of explanation.

Putting that plastic sticker on your boot was always a handy little escape from such potentially misguided branding. It said, 'OK, I don't have a Cornish number plate, but I'm very aware of it, and I want you to know that I'm Cornish, my car's

31

Cornish, and I bloody live here, all right?' Obviously it was completely unnecessary to employ a Kernow sticker if you had a Cornish number plate, because the people who mattered could already tell at a glance that you were local. That would be ridiculous. It was simply a device to be employed for the benefit of other locals, an almost subliminal nod, like the masons' handshake, unnoticed by those who didn't recognise it, but profoundly meaningful to a certain exclusive club.

I used to have a St Piran's Cross sewn on my backpack when I went abroad. I couldn't find any to buy back then, so had to get Mother to stitch me one. Wherever I went in the world it was amazing how often I met the same reaction. I'd like to say recognition and warm greetings, but alas it was never so. No, what I got was silence. Complete blankness. No-one ever asked about it, or mentioned it in any way. Eventually I concluded that with its vaguely religious look, maybe people thought I was promoting some sort of cult, and that I was perhaps on a pilgrimage they didn't like to ask about. I grew to like this. Looked at from a global perspective, St Piran is undeniably obscure, and it made me feel special.

Similarly during all the years I lived in London I had a Kernow sticker on the back of my motorbike helmet. You know, just in case. Should I ever come across another Cornish person up there, they'd immediately be left in no doubt as to my geographical and spiritual credentials. Occasionally I would spot another Cornish vehicle in London. On one occasion in the mid-eighties I saw a car in Putney which itself had a Kernow sticker! I drew up alongside it in a queue of traffic and lifted my visor. "Oggy Oggy Oggy!" I yelled excitedly at the attractive young female driver. She looked back at me, terrified. Maybe she'd borrowed the car.

The Kernow sticker was a subtle little sign back then. You didn't see one very often. But things have changed lately. A lot. Don't get me wrong, I'm all for the Cornish revivalists. Getting our language recognised under the European Charter for Regional or Minority Languages and the renaissance of Cornwall as an all-round desirable place to be are all good things in my opinion. But sometimes it feels like it's getting a little out of hand. And nowhere is this more apparent than in the blatant misuse of our Kernow sticker icon. I first noticed something was wrong a couple of years ago. I've got this friend. He's only lived in Cornwall a few years, and owns a car with a Cornish number plate. And one day there it was, on the boot, bold as you like. He's a very good friend, but there were several things that were wrong here. He'd only lived here a couple of years. The car was Cornish anyway. Just what was he trying to prove? I wanted to say, "But you've missed the whole point! The car's Cornish! You don't need one!" But for once I kept my mouth shut. I resolved simply to observe further.

Sure enough, when I looked, people were slapping them everywhere. I saw cars with more than one! I mentioned it to my wife who told me that she knows a couple who come down on holiday every year with a Kernow sticker on their car because they're convinced they get treated better by the locals. Like Canadian tourists who wear a maple leaf pin badge so we Brits don't mistake them for Americans and laugh at them. The biggest shock of all happened this summer when I spotted the classic Cornish holidaymaker, parked in a layby on a busy road, setting up his picnic table and pouring himself a cup of tea from a flask. He was scarlet with sunburn. And then I saw it, bold as you like, right there on the boot. Not even a nice subtle one either, but a big spangly affair, twice the size of the normal type. I felt a sinking sensation in the pit of my stomach as the reality dawned on me: the fact is, in 2003, the Kernow sticker has come to mean nothing more than, 'I've been to Cornwall, and I got this sticker'.

It got me thinking. Maybe the whole thing's always been a waste of time anyway. Since I've been driving I can't honestly remember an occasion when my displaying a Kernow sticker has had a noticeably positive effect. But I reckon there's still a strong case for wanting to exhibit our individuality. Judging by the type of vehicles you see every day, I'd say people are more concerned than ever about how they're perceived by others. We all want to be just a little bit individual. And with the current influx of people into Cornwall more and more locals want to display their Cornishness in some way. Especially since we can't even rely on our number plate to tell people we're Cornish any more. Our nice old familiar Cornish number plate prefixes were phased out in 2001. Since then all you get on your new car is a 'W' to denote 'West Country', with an 'R' or an 'L' after it. It's just not the same.

So what can we do, us Cornish drivers? How are we to declare our uniqueness now? I can only offer a couple of suggestions. The first is obvious. Get one of those number plates where the name of your local Cornish garage is printed on it at the bottom. A bit subtle I admit, because without binoculars, the average observer will never read it. Or you could just display an alternative type of sticker. There are certain districts in Cornwall where it's de rigeur to display a specific sticker anyway. You're no-one in St Agnes if you don't have a Lifeboats sticker on your car. You could have St Keverne Youth Band, Cornwall Knotweed Forum, Trepiddle Fuchsia Society, you name it. Have a Radio Cornwall one and you stand a chance of being spotted somewhere and winning their competition. Obviously you'll know not to fall into the trap of thinking a surfie sticker on your car means, 'I'm a Cornish surfer'. You're just as likely to see one in Milton Keynes.

At the end of the day if we Cornish are really concerned about asserting our identity on the road it's very easy. There's one thing you can do that will make your Cornishness abundantly clear to one an' all. Just drive a crappy old car.

Houseplants

2012

L et us consider for a moment the plight of the humble British houseplant. Bearing in mind that we pride ourselves on being a nation of both gardeners and animal lovers, you don't half see some manky specimens about the place.

I think our shameless neglect of houseplants may be due to the fact that so many species are amazingly resilient. They're practically asking for it. Take, say, the Devil's Ivy. That's a pretty common one. You see examples living in dark downstairs toilets throughout the country, surviving on little more than woodlice and air freshener. And who hasn't at one time been the proud owner of every student's favourite, a plant that seems to not only survive years with no moisture at all, but rewards such neglect by sending out cute little versions of itself on runners. I give you the Bear Grylls of houseplants, the spider plant.

I've been thinking about the life of the average British houseplant. We take a plant that should, by rights, be outside, somewhere in the world, enjoying itself. We position it in its pot, taking little account of light levels, humidity, all that boring stuff. The only thing we care about is that the plant now cunningly hides some ugly speaker cables, or an unsightly damp patch on the wall. We expect it to survive on whatever nutrients it can find in its pot, topped up every six months with the occasional half a glass of water when we're passing and the mood takes us. After a year or so we notice that it's only got five droopy leaves left on it, and we tut dismissively at the fact that it hasn't exactly become the architectural feature we'd planned. We resolve to give it a bit of a boost. After six months we remember, and at the garden centre our eye is caught by a new product you spray onto leaves to restore their shine. The product turns the five leaves so shiny it's hard to believe the plant was ever a natural thing at all. We confidently expect it to buck up now.

A few more months and we notice it's down to just the three leaves. Back to the garden centre for inspiration, and we buy some tomato food. To make up for lost time we up the dosage a bit and give it five times the recommended dose. The plant is now overloaded with nutrients that have been designed to make a tomato plant flower and fruit. Like a man dying of malnutrition trying to down a large bowl of banoffee pie, all the wrong elements are now creeping reluctantly round its sclerotic arteries.

Then one day we observe that it's lost its last leaf, and the sad little stem can no longer be described as remotely vertical. Better give it a water, we think. We give the parched dust in the pot a good soaking, finding an hour later that it's overflowed and soiled the lounge carpet. We curse the dead stick like a disgraced puppy and resentfully leave it to its own devices.

Two more months and we finally admit defeat when we find the dead stem lying on the floor. We empty the dry dust from the pot into the compost bin, experiencing a niggling sensation that perhaps things hadn't gone quite as well as they could have, but not really acknowledging any responsibility. 'Won't be getting one like that again,' we say to ourselves.

It's all very odd, this houseplant abuse. Maybe we should take a leaf out of the Dutch book. I was told by my local florist recently that in Holland they treat houseplants like cut flowers – as soon as one starts looking less than tip-top, they just chuck it out and get a new one. Those ruthless Dutch make no attempt to embrace them as a long term emotional commitment. We Brits prefer to think of an ailing houseplant like an elderly housebound relative. We know they aren't going to get significantly better, but, well, they're family.

You may be one of those rare people who genuinely takes an interest in your houseplants' welfare. If so, then I salute you. But chances are you've got a plant close to death within a few yards of where you're sitting. If so it's OK, you're quite normal.

Squirrel

2007

W e'll never need a TV in our kitchen. The garden is amply equipped with all manner of bird feeders, one of which is right outside the kitchen window. Come to think of it, our feathery friends have a wider choice of breakfast items than my wife and I. So most mornings we sit there and watch the show. But lately the show's become a little, well, *non-avian*.

Now I realise there are ways to tackle this old problem, from fancy squirrel-proof devices (which, in my experience, just make our fluffy friends all the more devious), to diversionary, bespoke squirrel feeding stations positioned at the opposite end of the garden from the birdies' preferred dining area. But no matter what I've tried over the years, all I've got is more damn squirrels. This morning there were three of them tucking in while the poor tits and finches peeped out from behind the foliage, chirping anxiously to disguise their rumbling tummies, and longingly licking their beaks.

Not that I used to mind that much. I'd simply marvel at Mr Squirrel's cheeky, muscular agility. His antics can be breathtaking as he performs his twitchy, death-defying leaps and twists one minute, only to become a comical, freeze-frame statue the next. If I'm honest, I've always found them quite cute, despite the argument that they're just rats with fluffy tails.

But things are getting out of hand now. For one thing I'm worried the kitchen window will soon be shattered, such is the force with which Mr Squirrel launches himself from the feeder, across the lawn and up a tree every time he detects the slightest alien movement in the kitchen (the glinting of the kettle usually does it). The other day the bang of feeder against window was so loud I thought a low flying buzzard must have hit it. But looking at the bigger picture, the fact is that there's nothing good about the grey squirrel. They are bark-stripping, sap-sucking, nest-robbing, electric cable-shredding, timber-vandalising, ASBO-deserving little yobs. Worst of all is the fact that they are bigger, tougher, hardier, uglier and, well, *greyer* than our sweet little red version, whose butt they've been spending the past hundred or so years kicking (not literally, obviously, although it's a poignant image). We Brits love a loser, and a red squirrel is certainly one of those.

Of course it's not the grey squirrel's fault. To him it's just survival. He didn't maliciously gatecrash our little party island just to cause trouble. He wasn't to know we preferred our trees with their bark on, not ripped open, oozing sap until they've lost the will to live. No, it's the blind tenacity of the shortsighted Victorians at whom we should be jabbing our accusational finger. It was no easy feat, believe it or not, but their determination to infest Britain with these pesky grey intruders drove them to release and re-release more and more, until they were confident that they'd started breeding. So now we're left with a classic example of the results of introducing non-native species into a country.

Not that we're the only country to suffer like this. Look at the European rabbit's invasion of the New World. Or the introduction of a few Australian possums into New Zealand, where there are now an estimated eighty million of the blighters, wiping out countless vulnerable little flightless native birds. We should count ourselves lucky that it is mostly the red squirrel that the grey has put paid to. So far.

On the positive side, there are places in the world that have held out against such onslaughts; Tasmania has resisted the European red fox's invasion of Australia, just as our Isle of Wight has resisted the grey squirrel's invasion of Britain. Which got me thinking – here in Cornwall we consider ourselves a proud people, spiritually and even physically independent of our English oppressors to the east, partly due to the presence of that natural boundary, the majestic Tamar. It's been well-documented that squirrels can swim, but this is certainly not its preferred way of getting around. I don't think a squirrel has ever swum if it could help it. And they can't fly, obviously. Oh sure they can jump, but not that far. It would certainly have had a problem at Plymouth. But at the weak points further up, where Cornish shores flirt dangerously close to those of our Devonian neighbours, what itinerant squirrel could have resisted the temptation to leap for all it was worth, or even throw itself into the murky depths, in search of a better life out west?

Now this is undeniably a case of bolting the stable door after the red squirrel has bolted, but surely had we widened the Tamar a little in places a couple of hundred years ago instead of putting all that effort into building bridges and ferries, well, we might all be a lot better off. Not to mention standing proud as one of the last true British sanctuaries of the much lamented *Sciurus vulgaris*. Just a thought.

Health scare

2008

I recently became hooked on the TV series *Doc Martin*, and I'm feeling rather ambivalent about the whole thing. For anyone who hasn't seen it, this is a sort of comedy drama about a top London surgeon whose blood phobia necessitates a move to a remote seaside village to work as a GP. Here he encounters an array of colourful local characters who are, by turns, eccentric, naïve, small-minded, or just plain thick. Of course they are. This is primetime telly, and this is the countryside. Everyone's an idiot in the country, we all know that. Particularly the West Country. It's a given in TV sitcoms that Londoners are villains, northerners are lovably blunt, Scottish people are tight, Welsh people complain a lot and people from the West Country are stupid. And a bit weird.

But as a Cornishman I wasn't that offended when I started watching *Doc Martin*, because at least it wasn't set in Cornwall. Or so I thought. I just assumed it was set somewhere else, like Dorset, or Somerset, or somewhere. Somewhere with very odd-sounding accents anyway. It was plainly filmed in Port Isaac, since every time anyone steps out of a house the familiar seascape is very recognisable (the doctor's house, the policeman's house, the schoolteacher's house, the plumber's house, the school, they're all right on the harbour). I just assumed that things must be quite old-fashioned like this in Dorset, which is plainly a county with coastal villages where public sector workers can afford houses by the harbour, and actually live in them. All year round. You know, like they did in Cornwall in the olden days.

But then something strange happened. After an episode or two I began to notice references to Delabole, and Truro. And I realised to my amazement that this programme was, in fact, supposed to be an actual, modern day Cornish fishing village. And these bizarre accents were supposed to sound *Cornish*! So here was a pretty Cornish fishing village with no gridlocked traffic, where the beach is constantly populated by swarthy fishermen, every local has a hilarious secret, the lovable local bobby is an idiot yet keeps his job, and a plumber can become a restaurateur overnight using a man he met in the street as head chef, the houses have people living in them, and the schoolkids sit on lobsterpots on the beach for their lessons. Nice. This is chocolate box, paint-by-numbers Cornwall.

I realise it's obviously only light entertainment, but I've got very mixed feelings about our world being portrayed in this way. Do people upcountry in 2008 really think any aspect of this portrayal could be realistic? If so they must get some shock when they actually come and visit. It wouldn't matter if they were presenting it as a fictitious county. But it is clearly saying that this is 21st century Cornwall. Perhaps it doesn't matter. Perhaps it only matters that it looks nice, which it does.

It's all very odd, and yet I'm hooked on it. The show works, above all else, not because of the scenery, or the quirky locals, or the rather lovely schoolteacher. It works because of the doctor himself who, despite his lacking any semblance of bedside manner, is quite brilliant. If a heavily pregnant woman arrives on the scene, you know he's going to be whipping a healthy baby out on a cliff top somewhere with seconds to spare before the end of the episode. He's happy to try a bit of medieval trepanning by taking a power drill to somebody's skull, and he's no stranger to an emergency tracheostomy. All he needs is an old biro and something with which to make a hole in the patient's neck. Doc Martin is, truly, the best doctor in the history of doctoring. Every episode features a mysterious ague to which the good Doc applies his mighty brain, and every time his diagnosis is spot on. And this is certainly a sickly village. A village with this many problems would by rights have a *British Medical Journal* columnist permanently on site to write groundbreaking articles about its latest outbreak. But of course such a person would have to live right on the harbour, because that's where everyone lives, and unfortunately all those £600,000 houses are already taken by tradesmen and public sector workers.

I'll say one thing for the show. It does make for entertaining telly. And let's face it, it's set in Cornwall, and it does seem people can't get enough of the place. I'm sure there will always be an audience for *Doc Martin*. It might misrepresent us, and be a bit lightweight, and a bit silly, but hey, nobody's perfect.

Retro caravan

2011

A s spring approaches, and one's mind turns to pleasurable warm weather pursuits, I'm worried that something odd is happening to me. Maybe it's a midlife crisis.

First I sold my beautiful motorcycle. Then it occurred to me one Saturday night that I was perfectly happy, no, *relieved*, to be staying in and not going down the pub. And now this. A powerful and very real urge to acquire a caravan. Not any old caravan though.

Nobody can deny that caravans are useful. You're in a weatherproof, insulated shell, which means you can go camping without being at the mercy of the one thing that all too often ruins life under canvas. And you can unhook it and drive to all sorts of places in your car, making it far more versatile, on a long trip, than a gas-guzzling, lane-clogging, unwieldy campervan.

But unless they actually own one, nobody actually likes caravans, do they? I know I don't. They're certainly not attractive. And our wretched memories of A30 villages like Mitchell and Fraddon, clogged with nose-to-tail white boxes preventing locals from going about their business, are hard to erase. Although those pre-bypass days are long gone, caravans will always have a certain stigma.

People laugh at caravans. Always have. The sneering clever dicks of BBC's *Top Gear* will never understand that there are road users out there who are in no particular hurry, who enjoy looking at the scenery, and, worst of all, don't seem to care that others are annoyed by this. Caravans are always going to get up the noses of those more concerned with getting from A to B in the fastest possible time.

So, why am I suddenly so interested in getting one? Simple. It's because I've discovered a new type of caravan. Or, more accurately, an old type. Through no fault of my own, I've found myself flirting with the world of *retro caravans*. My epiphany occurred last summer while camping down west. We were in the tent section of the campsite, as usual. Walking to the ablutions hut one evening, there it was, in among all the boring white modern boxes. It was small, it was roundish, it was built in the fifties. The owners had decked it out with sweet little bespoke window boxes, and bunting, and all sorts of lovely period touches. Inside, everything was perfectly in its place. Little bunk beds had been fitted for the kids. The owners were, well, for want of a better word, just plain cool. Young, outdoorsy, friendly, they couldn't have cared less what people thought of them. I liked that.

This caravan was pleasing in every way: all clean, round shapes and swooping lines on the outside, all melamine cupboards and wood trim and neat little catches and cubbyholes on the inside. A sad minority of our society might mock a retro caravan, as they might mock a ginger-haired girl, but they are completely missing the plain truth that these are frequently things of breathtaking beauty. I want one. The caravan I mean.

Depending on whom you talk to, it's easy to believe that retro caravans could be the next big thing. You can, after all, still pick them up relatively cheaply, just as you used to occasionally stumble upon a tatty but salvageable classic car, languishing under a tarpaulin in an old hay barn. And one of the best things about retro caravans is that they aren't really vehicles at all, are they? So you get none of those inconvenient, oily shenanigans that come with a classic car.

I don't think I'm having a midlife crisis; I think I'm facing up to a few things. My desire to own a classic retro caravan is the same as my stubborn refusal to throw away my *Herb Alpert and the Tijuana Brass* LPs. It's time to stop hiding them every time someone under thirty comes round. I like these things. I just do. If this is a midlife crisis, bring it on.

I probably won't drive anywhere with my retro caravan though. I'll just put it in the garden and look at it.

Pasty

2006

T he other day I mentioned to someone that I write a column for a Cornish magazine. "Oh right," they replied. "What's that all about then, pasties and things I suppose."

At first I felt vaguely insulted that of all the pressing issues facing us in Cornwall, all the subjects that need to be discussed, the pasty was the first thing this person could think of. Never mind our unemployment. Never mind the deficit at Treliske hospital. Forget our exhorbitant house prices. Such condescending ignorance reminded me of another time when I heard a northerner expressing bemused surprise that there are mines of any description in Cornwall. But then it got me thinking; actually I don't ever write about hard-hitting issues anyway – I leave things like that to proper journalists, so I can write about flowers and choughs and the funny things that holidaymakers do. And actually I don't think I have ever mentioned pasties in the hallowed pages of this fine organ. And I do actually have something to say about them. Just this once. So here goes.

It seems to me there's a paradox when it comes to pasties. An *ingrediential dialectic* if you will. It goes as follows: most Cornish people have traditionally always proclaimed something along the lines of, 'Oh yes, pasties are most versatile.

You'm put anything in a pasty, boy'. And of course this is true: it's the whole point of a pasty. A couple of hundred years ago you'd have been very happy to pop a bit of rabbit in there if there was some spare, or some pork if, say, your neighbour had killed a pig recently. Failing that, a bit of cheese or an egg would suffice to provide protein. You couldn't afford to be that fussy. Although I can't find much evidence to support the claim that miners' wives put the savoury up one end and some fruit for afters down the other, and my grandmother, born in Mitchell in 1906, has never heard of such practices, there's no doubt that they'd certainly have made separate fruity pasties. They'd have been mad not to, with the September hedgerows groaning with blackberries, and the trees laden with apples.

And yet, as soon as the well-meaning rookie pasty maker tentatively and respectfully begins listing the ingredients they've used for their first adventure into the world of Cornish cuisine, the critical Cornishperson sits there snobbily, fingers drumming table, eyebrows raised incredulously, poised to pounce upon the first mistake. And when the poor fellow commits that foulest of offences, well, all hell breaks loose. The conversation commonly goes something like this:

Person attempting first pasty: "So I rolled out some pastry..."

Cornish sceptic, sucking air in through tightly pursed lips: "Oh yes..."

"...And then I put in some finely chopped potato…"

"Mm hmm…"

"......and some onion...."

"Yes…"

50

"...and a bit of carrot..."

"What?!" comes the horrified Cornish response. "You put carrot....*in a pasty*!!!? No!!!! You can't do that! that ent a proper pasty!! Not.......with........*carrot*!!!"

Pity the non-Cornish pasty maker who so much as glazes the pastry with a bit of milk, for the wrath of all Trelawny's army shall rain down upon them. It's as if the Cornishperson is worried that their Cornish authenticity is in doubt if they don't show themselves to defend the sacredness of the four divine ingredients: beef skirt, potato, onion and turnip. It's true they do go fantastically well together, but you can't blame people for wanting to vary it a bit. TV chefs have tried it on a fairly regular basis, I'm told. Bless 'em, they're plainly trying to justify their existence by making a dish using more than four ingredients, but you can guarantee the BBC phone lines are jammed by irate Cornish folk screaming, "The seasoning must be plain salt and pepper, nothing else! How can you use low sodium rock salt?! It's...not...the...*same*!"

If you think about it, the controversy surrounding our pasty befits its status. After all it's Cornwall's contribution to world cuisine, so no wonder people get defensive. I can't think of many examples of homegrown regional fast food that is commonly available on the other side of the world. What else is there? Yorkshire pudding? Eccles cakes? Welsh Rarebit? Not the same really, is it? Never mind the embarrassing fact that a pasty from your average Australian pie shop way surpasses the vile processed plasticised mess that passes for one in many British shops and garages. The fact is we invented it, and a proper pasty, made by a Cornish grandmother, in Cornwall, is as good as it gets.

So let's hold our pasties aloft, and be proud of what we've achieved. Let's all keep the dream alive and make pasties within the next few weeks. Go on, you know it's been ages. And don't be ashamed of whatever you choose to put in there. After all, that's often how great recipes are invented – cooks who haven't quite got the right ingredient grabbing something else that's to hand.

No carrots though. That would just be weird.

Audrey's leg

2004

You may recall that three years ago my wife and I got geese. There were two main reasons:

1) To graze on the grass on our top field, which I was fed up with mowing.

2) To see if we coped with the responsibility well enough to embrace the more ambitious world of the smallholder.

Well, I can categorically state that it's been lovely having them. Our geese happily munch away on the field, give a rural feel to the place, supply us with eggs, and provide a convenient 'doorbell' facility when anyone approaches. But over three years have gone by now, and what have we done? Just how many more creatures have we added to our smallholding after all this time? Well, just some chickens, actually. No Vietnamese pot-bellied pigs. No alpacas. Not even a modest goat. We're no closer to being proper smallholders than we were back then. The reason? Because we're just too soft. Allow me to explain.

Audrey is one of our geese. She's the youngest and the lightest, and came to us quite recently from the RSPCA, who'd found her staggering around a cabbage field, alone, somewhere near Penzance. No-one knew how she got there, but we were quite happy to take her. I doubt geese are entitled to nine lives like a cat, but they obviously get more than one, because Audrey had used one up already, and was soon to need another.

Every year, after they go through their summer moult, we have to clip each goose's wing, the idea being that this prevents them from attempting to get airborne and potentially hurting themselves. We recognised this as a necessity after a near miss with one of them in the early days, and it's worked nicely now for three years. Despite having a majestic wingspan and resembling quite closely many types of wild goose, the domestic goose was not bred for efficient flight. So it's for their own good.

But alas this year we were a bit tardy with the annual wing-clipping ritual. They moulted, grew their splendid new wing feathers, and I kept meaning to get out there and do the job. And then it was too late. One afternoon I was sitting in my little office, tapping away on the computer much as I am now, when I heard a very loud, yet ominously soft, thud on the roof. Like a piano stool wrapped in three eiderdowns, dropped from a height. I sat there for a few seconds, wondering whether to stand up and investigate. But my bewilderment paled compared to that of Audrey, who I then spotted out of the window. She'd evidently now fallen off the roof to land on the steps, and was sitting, stunned, with her right leg sticking out at an angle that didn't look very comfortable at all.

It was at this point that I immediately knew I'd never be anything more than a soft-hearted, well, pet owner. Any self-respecting smallholder would have taken one look at her and thought, 'Ah well, that's Sunday lunch taken care of'. I'm sure David Archer would have reached straight for a broom handle and some old newspapers (I've read up about the technique – I'll spare you the details. Actually I've upset myself even thinking about it). Twenty years ago maybe that could have been me. Twenty years ago I could shoot a rabbit. These days I just want to cuddle them. Friends tell me it's since I met my vegetarian, humanitarian wife, but the fact is I'd been a bunny-hugger for a long time before that. So when I looked at Audrey lying there, vulnerable, in pain, without a friend in the world, I could only think one thing. And it wasn't cranberry sauce. Or whatever you have with goose.

So I headed with Audrey straight to the vet's. On the way there all sorts of prognoses filled my imagination. A goose isn't really one of those birds that can get by hopping about on just the one leg, like the occasional manky town pigeon you see. They're a bit lardy for that kind of caper. I had visions of Audrey with a little wooden leg, perhaps fashioned from a small girl's skipping rope handle. If gangrene set in then both handles could be utilised for the full Douglas Bader effect. Or perhaps her stump could be strapped to a little skateboard wheel, and she'd bravely learn to get around on it and conquer her disability, and eventually be featured on one of those TV shows hosted by Esther Rantzen, celebrating the indomitable nature of the human spirit. And the, er, goose one. They'd make Audrey's story into a movie, and I'd write the screenplay, after all there was that famous goose movie about the little girl and her dad who teach that flock of snow geese to fly, wasn't there, so that proves there's a market for goose-based feature films. I could start a genre. But wait a minute, I was getting carried away. All I could hope for, realistically, was that the leg could be saved.

Arriving at the vet's with a damn great goose under your arm is a bit of a double-edged sword. Part of you feels pretty cool; there's an undeniable kudos about standing there with what many people assume to be quite a scary animal under your arm. Maybe not quite as hard as turning up with a hyena on a chain, but getting there. Course you don't let on that they're really soft as can be. There's also the novelty factor of standing in a room where 95% of the patients are doggies and moggies, and you've got this, well, farm animal. I told the attractive young receptionist what had happened and then the animal's name.

"Audrey."

"And your surname?"

"Cross."

I saw her write Audrey Cross on the form. All the kudos was gone. I made no attempt to feel cool now. Now I felt ridiculous.

The vet called us in. He examined Audrey and suggested keeping her in, doing an x-ray, and possibly giving her a general anesthetic so they could put a pin in her leg. At this point the vet (ignoring the fact that Audrey was doing her best to take a decent chunk out of his forearm) looked knowingly into my eyes and said, sympathetically, "I'm assuming she's really a pet."

"Yes," I mumbled, looking at the floor. "Don't worry about the money. Just do whatever it takes." The vet had seen it all before. It's what being British is all about, isn't it? A completely irrational, and wildly variable, obsession with the welfare of animals. It's probably true that if it was a Hereford bull requiring a triple heart bypass I might have given a little more thought to what the final bill might amount to. But all I wanted was Audrey back, ideally with full use of her legs. And damn the expense!

I was thus confronted with the brutal realisation that I was nothing more than a namby pamby goose-hugger. Not a smallholder, simply a pet owner with delusions of grandeur. I said goodbye to Audrey, who was now officially an inpatient, and reassured her that I'd call in the morning. As I left the vet's, there was a tough-looking tattooed man sitting in reception with one of those scary terriers, and he looked at me. I wanted to say, "I had a goose under my arm when I arrived you know. A big one".

Next morning on the phone they told me that Audrey had a badly fractured femur, and that they'd put a pin in. I picked her up later that day, and there followed weeks of to-ing and fro-ing to the vet for checkups and to have the pin taken out, while I kept Audrey in solitary confinement away from her three friends who, to be honest, didn't really look all that concerned. After two months she was hardly limping at all. The pin was removed, then another week's wait, and then finally she was ready to rejoin her pals. As I watched them grazing together, behaving as if nothing had happened, I reflected on the events of the previous couple of months. Six trips to and from the vet (a 25 mile round trip), all that anxiety, and a final bill of, wait for it, no I just can't bring myself to admit it. OK, *a hundred and fifty pounds*. There, I said it. Obviously a goose can't talk, but she didn't even look the slightest bit grateful. In fact she keeps trying to bite me.

Now I'll be the first to say that the vet did a superb job, and I feel I totally got my money's worth. In fact in 'Ripoff Britain' I reckon the vet's bill represented pretty good value, considering. Having said that, I've related Audrey's tale to various people, and have experienced very mixed reactions. Some say, "You big softies, are you going to rush to the vets every time one of your geese has a runny bottom?" And some say, "I'd have done the same, don't you worry." But incredibly, it seems that a one hundred and fifty pound vet's bill is, well, chicken feed to many pet owners. Two friends in London admitted to me recently that they had just parted with fifteen hundred pounds to pay for their cat's dental bill. No, you don't have to go back and re-read it, I'll say it again: *fifteen hundred pounds to pay for their cat's dental bill.*

Personally I like to think I'd have had the courage to furnish the vet with a decent pair of long-nose pliers and introduce my gummy new cat to a brave new world of drinking straws and slightly watered-down Kit-e-Kat. I mean, how bad could life be for a toothless moggy in a loving home? Now I'm sure there are those of you who are probably thinking that it's OK to spend a fortune on a cat, because it's a proper pet. Not like a goose. Well you'd be wrong. The fact that some people are too narrow-minded to look at a goose without thinking of Christmas is not my problem. Just because you can't watch EastEnders with a goose on your lap doesn't make it a less worthy companion. I mean, you wouldn't let your pedigree thoroughbred into the front room either, but some people are very attached to their horses. It's all relative. You can't draw a line. These days if someone tells me their vet charged them fifty quid to put a splint on their stick insect, I'm all sympathy.

But I'm definitely starting to appreciate why everyone's getting pet insurance. I've always held out against such a spurious luxury because it seemed like an indulgence, symptomatic of today's obsession with insurance and security. But in the light of my recent experiences I'm definitely starting to see the advantages of appropriate insurance in certain areas. I'm going to look into it.

But I do have my limits. If Audrey ever tries using up another life and expects me to foot the bill again, and it's a bit closer to Christmas, well, you never know.

Christmas

2005

Oh dear, the season of goodwill is upon us again. As always, the media will be inducing mass panic with stories of it being either the busiest retail period ever, or the quietest, and we'll be bombarded with information about how the average British family spends £23,000 on presents and will be in debt until 2039 as a result. I'm fed up with it. These days it seems any notion of goodwill to all men, let alone the celebration of the birth of someone significant, has given way to a blinding wave of shallow materialism, commercialisation and the worship of extremely false idols. "Ah, but we do it for the children," they say. Well not when the children are baying like rabid dogs for this year's TV-hyped electrical must-have, or American movie-based doll. All cannon fodder for the 2010 car boot sale. Clearly, something's rotten in Santa's grotto.

That story about Coca Cola inventing Santa upset me. OK, not inventing exactly, but changing his outfit. The story goes that the only reason Santa's garb is red and white is because an illustrator changed it from the traditional green to match the Coke branding for their advertisements. In the 1930s. That's how long this sort of thing's been going on. We're all to blame. I myself can even remember impatiently demanding an Action Man with realistic gripping hands for Christmas. None of your quaint old rigid-digitted military dolls for me, not once I'd embraced the oh-so-seductive grippy metatarsals of the new, er, 'digitally enhanced' model, if you'll excuse the pun. Observing the meaningful way in which my best friend Ern's Action Man could hold a grenade, the green-eyed monster reared up in me and that was it. So I'm as guilty as anybody. I know I should have been happy with a satsuma and a couple of mouldy walnuts, like my grandparents would have been. Nobody is without blame. We are all culpable. Christmas brings out the worst in all of us.

That said, all is not lost. Far from it. For the Yuletide represents a unique opportunity to celebrate a most wonderful thing. It's the one thing that sets our nation apart from the rest of the world. No, not the total collapse of our manufacturing industries. Not the demise of subsidised dental care, nor the extinction of indigenous British cuisine. It's good, old-fashioned British eccentricity I'm talking about. There is simply no period on the calendar quite like Christmas for forcing us to indulge in a frenzy of ludicrous behaviour that at any other time of the year would be deemed certifiable. The average chap, for example, spends hundreds of pounds on inappropriate gifts for people who already have too much stuff, and the recipients do the same to him. He also wastes half a tree's worth of card sending a pseudo-religious message to dozens of people he hasn't been in touch with since he did the same thing a year before. And again, they do the same thing back. Christmas brings it all out. Utter lunacy. He has a few days off work so he eats and drinks to excess, starting the new year bloated and regretful. He'll spend an entire day speeding between relatives in Falmouth, Crackington Haven, Sennen, Delabole and Falmouth, all given exactly equal gift-opening time so as not to cause family ructions. Especially if he's married. Then he'll take to a freezing moor, or perhaps a rain-lashed windswept beach, clad in hopelessly inappropriate clothing, all in the name of 'blowing away the cobwebs'. And then he might, if he's a true eccentric, take things up a notch. A nice dip in the Atlantic, that's just the ticket.

We wouldn't have it any other way, would we? Ridiculous as it all is, I know very few people who've rejected this crazy festival, religious or otherwise. And the reason? Because we love it. It's all curiously life affirming. So as you struggle up that ladder to string up another couple of hundred quid's worth of illuminated plastic reindeer, and rush down the shops wielding as many credit cards as your wheelbarrow will carry, just remember that no matter how mad it all seems, in another twelve months, you're going to be doing it all over again.

Fishy epiphany

2008

W hat's the most unusual fish you've ever eaten?

With decreasing stocks and increasing air mile guilt, we're constantly being encouraged to embrace local ingredients which we'd previously have turned our noses up at. And slowly the teachings of people like Hugh Fearnley-Whitting-stall are having an effect on us. When we step outside our gastronomic comfort zone we often find the unlikeliest things quite delicious. So, like the reluctant child who tries a bit of broccoli, and realises it's not so bad, our minds are broadened. It is surely a good thing.

Often our reluctance is due to sheer revulsion at the very sight of the poor beast. If an animal is ugly, or just unfamiliar-looking, then to many people it will be, by definition, unappetising. Take monkfish. You can't deny that it's a seriously ugly fish (unless you're another monkfish). I wouldn't be surprised if the first time a human ever came face to face with one they simply said, "OK I'm hungry, but I'm not *that* hungry". The same thing with red gurnard. But now, at last, the odd-looking but delicious monkfish and gurnard are becoming much sought after. As my old school motto says: 'To be, and not to seem to be'. Or, I suppose, 'Never judge a monkfish by the fact that it looks like something off Doctor Who'. I expect the Germans have a word for this phenomenon, this culinary epiphany which happens when you discover that something you previously discarded as ugly and inedible is, in fact, very tasty indeed.

I'm not so sure about grey mullet though. I wouldn't exactly call it an ugly fish, but it's a fish that lives in ugly places. Whenever you're sitting on a harbour wall, or by a muddy estuary, and you suddenly hear someone shout "Wow! Look at these fish! They're huge!" it's usually grey mullet they're looking at. These big-scaled beasts cruise along the bottom, devouring all manner of mud-dwelling organic detritus, daring you to have a go. And people tend not to, because it's notoriously tricky to catch one, and you wouldn't know what to do with it if you did. That's because they've always been considered rubbish eating. But now we're being told that even the grey mullet is good to eat. In fact it seems it's not far from joining its far nobler red cousin (actually they are not related at all), and no self-respecting, sustainable, 21st century fish cookbook is complete without a couple of recipes.

I tried cooking grey mullet for my inlaws once, and the putrid mess I ended up with was literally inedible. In the circumstances I decided honesty was the best policy, held my hands up and announced to my guests, "This is absolutely disgusting. It looks, smells and tastes awful, and we're not eating it." With a theatrical flourish that I hoped would reduce the shame, I flung the entire dish in the bin, apologised again, and set about cooking something else instead. The recipe was from a certain highly respected fish chef's book out of which

I've made lots of lovely things in the past, so I can only assume the fault must have lain with me, or with the provenance of the fish. It may have been all my fault, but it'll be a while before I go near a grey mullet again.

The poor old spider crab hasn't quite made the transition yet either. These long-legged, knobbly, deep-sea beasties have long been considered weird, inedible, and fit only for bait and the French. We either throw them back or pack them off to the continent, but we certainly don't spend any time eating them. The Spanish apparently revere these '*centolla*' more than lobster. I'd love to try one, but it seems in the UK they will forever be consigned to a status several notches below the more traditional 'edible' brown crab. These days you do occasionally hear of someone extolling their virtues, but you'd be lucky to find one in a fishmonger's or in anything but the most progressive seafood restaurant.

My favourite example of all culinary epiphanies is the humble dogfish. I well remember throwing countless 'spurdog' back whilst fishing off Newquay in the sixties and seventies. For us to ever consider this sandpaper-skinned pauper of a fish worth a taste, Mr Dogfish was going to need a serious marketing job. And that's what he got. They rebranded him, gave him a new identity. Whichever marketing genius hilariously renamed him *rock salmon*, I'd like to shake him by the hand, just for his sheer front. Apparently the same consultant rebranded potatoes as *subterranean truffle tubers* the same year, but it never caught on. OK I made that bit up. But I did read recently about a classy Vietnamese restaurant in

London listing the eels on its menu as 'Vietnamese long fish' in the assumption that punters would prefer to pay for something exotic and foreign than a plateful of those slippery, snakey things they'd just seen in the Thames on the way to the restaurant.

Just think what a good time we could have been having all these years, if only we weren't such slaves to our gastronomic inhibitions. All those rock salmon we threw back in the seventies. It rather makes you wonder what abhorrent dish we'll be tucking into with gusto this time next year after experiencing another unexpected revelation.

Tender fillet of garlic slow worm on crostini anyone?

Telegram

2006

E agle-eyed readers may have noticed, a couple of months ago, that I nonchalantly mentioned I'd been chatting to my Cornish grandmother, who was born in 1906. And those of you who didn't, like me, fail maths O level on more occasions than we are capable of counting, may even have cleverly worked out that she should be turning a hundred around now. Well, you'd be right. She's now a hundred and a bit.

It was quite an experience, Nan's hundredth. "Nan's practically a centurian!" I remember saying to my wife. "I think you mean *centenarian*," she corrected, pityingly. "Unless you've seen her ordering a hundred Roman soldiers about lately." Back when Nan was in her late nineties, you didn't dare hope that she would ever reach the target. As the cautious buildup began, it became more of a reality, and we began to make all sorts of discoveries. The first surprise was that turning a hundred these days is not that big a deal. Seems there are bucketfuls of centenarians about the place. I did a bit of research. Twenty years ago there were only 300 or so in the UK. Now it's more like 6,000. In another twenty? I can think of a few Cornish villages where they might be in the majority by then. And it is presumably for this reason that you don't even get the coveted Royal telegram automatically. I'm not sure if

Buckingham Palace are hoping a few of the 6,000 people a year might slip through the net and save them a few quid, but the sad fact is that you're actually required to apply for the thing beforehand, otherwise you won't get one. Furthermore they're not interested in your application until three weeks before the event, which, I suppose, is fair enough when you bear in mind the statistical odds against the subject hanging in there for a further three weeks. We felt bad about laughing, but no-one could deny that there was a touch of black comedy in the way the letter from Buckingham Palace emphasised in no uncertain terms that *'Should circumstances relating to this anniversary alter in any way, such as change of address, would you please notify the Anniversaries Officer'*. We speculated on what the postcode of this new address might be. HEV 1N, hopefully.

The big day approached, and I found myself wondering about it all. The whole thing's a bit strange really. When someone turns a hundred, what exactly are we all celebrating? Surely it's just the fact that they're still alive, when most people keel over a fair bit sooner. When you hunt down that elusive card with a big *100* on the front (there aren't many about, believe me), and you go to write something appropriate inside, it's hard to come up with a sentence which isn't a thinly disguised, *'Congratulations! Statistically you really should have died quite a while ago. So well done, because none of us thought you'd make it!'* There's no denying that it's quite an achievement, but unless you've actually been dedicating yourself to maximising your own longevity, I'm just not sure how appropriate congratulations really are.

And another thing started to bother me. After we've all celebrated that big, round, one hundred, how are we supposed to treat the occasion a year on, if the person is lucky enough to turn 101? An undeniably less appealing number, but statistically surely it is a far greater achievement. Tricky one this. If you get a telegram from Her Majesty on your hundredth, I'd say a bunch of flowers is in order on your 101st, and a personal visit by the time you reach 102.

On the day, things went very nicely. Nan sat there serenely while we family members ran round organising tea and cake and champagne. We even hired a brass band, because she likes a brass band, does Nan. And what of the telegram? Did it arrive? Of course it did. A day early, actually, on account of Nan's birthday being on a Sunday, and the fact that it's not actually a telegram these days, but a big card that just comes in the post. But it had a big Buck Palace postmark, which looks really impressive, and gold tassels, and a lovely message, and a signature that is so well printed you'd swear it was the real thing. I don't think it mattered that it came in the common old Royal Mail. You'd have to be a hundred to remember what a telegram was anyway.

I concluded that the whole thing hasn't really got much to do with reaching an arbitrary number of years. What we are celebrating is the life itself, no matter how long. It is the quality, and not the quantity of days spent walking the earth that count. Your Mozarts achieve everything by the time they hit thirty. Some need a hundred years to do it all. At Nan's hundredth we were saying, "Wow, we're so glad to still have you around, and it's a privilege to still be able to spend time with someone who can hold us spellbound with descriptions of rural Cornish life in the 1920s. Someone who is still smiling after living through polio and two World Wars". We were celebrating knowing Nan. Her turning a hundred was really just a bonus.

Scilly

2006

B y the time my wife and I arrived on one of Scilly's off islands for our much-needed winter holiday, we were getting seriously concerned. It wasn't the ominous tone of our prospective landlady's voice as I booked the holiday let weeks earlier: "You do realise there's only a skeleton boat service between the islands," she informed me. "It's not at all like summer."

"No problem at all," I gaily replied, looking forward to the solitude, the wildness, the, oh let's be honest, *exclusivity*.

Hugh Town on St Mary's was the first hint of what was to come. Although admittedly there was no tumbleweed blowing down the high street, and the person who stepped out of the Co-op at noon was a little old lady with a tartan shopping trolley and not Gary Cooper, the place had a quiet and eery atmosphere. Then we noticed the obvious elation in the local teenagers' voices as we overheard them describing to each other the fashion items they'd managed to get delivered by buying them on the internet.

But it was only when we hopped off the boat at our chosen island destination that the full reality of winter holidaying in Scilly became apparent to us. There was no doubt in our minds that this was going to be interesting.

The only pub on the island overlooks the quay, and, considering it has no competition, is far nicer than anyone has any right to expect. Many a balmy summer's evening I've wiled away there in the past, drinking good brown beer, admiring the fine ladies of the gig teams as they stopped off for sundowners, and tucking into divine fish suppers. Obviously we realised that the thronging hordes of visitors were now long gone, and that the pub would probably not be providing quite the service that the August visitor might expect. But we confidently hoped to stroll down there of an evening for a glass of ale and perhaps a rudimentary meal of some kind, maybe even occasionally involving a bit of fresh fish. Heck, Scilly had even acquired its own brewery since we'd last visited.

And so as we stepped off the boat and set foot on the hallowed slipway, and gazed up at the venerated cob walls of my dream pub, and collared the first local we happened upon, I gingerly enquired as to its winter opening times. Gazing intently skywards, his eyes narrowing to slits, lips pursed, he concentrated hard. At this I smelled a rat. I mean, it was the only pub on the island. Wouldn't you know the opening hours if that was you? And finally came the reason: "I believe they might be opening at eight thirty on Wednesday evening," he proclaimed.

And so the template for the following week was set. The pub was shut, the 'skeleton' boat service was more like a shinbone and a couple of metatarsals of a service, and there were literally no other visitors on the island. Well, apart from a rather dishevelled woman who emerged early one morning with walking boots and a backpack looking for all the world as though she'd slept in a hedge.

And you know what? It was one of the best holidays we've ever had. And this is because everything you go to Scilly for in the summer is intensified in the winter. Apart from the temperature, obviously. Peace? It's even more peaceful. Scenery? The sea is just as blue and the landscape has less people to get in the way. Just a few less plants in flower. Lovely old-fashioned, crime-free atmosphere? More so, with less people to commit crimes, not that anyone ever has in Scilly. Friendly? Even friendlier because the exasperated locals aren't spending the days having the same conversation with every visitor about how lucky they are to live in such a beautiful place and what's it like in the winter?

And so you slip into a daily routine of walks, and beachcombing, and chats about whether you could live here. Oh, and that most essential of Scilly tourist occupations: sussing out who's who on the island, who's related to whom, whose family has lived here for five hundred years, and who's only lived here for a season or two and speculating as to whether they're running away from some dark secret, and what that secret might be. And on Wednesday the pub opens, and it's brilliant because there's a quiz on, and you're the only visitors, and that's the way most of us want a holiday to be. By the end of the week you think you know all about everyone. But of course you don't. You know nothing. Just the few bits people have allowed you to know. And that's partly what makes you want to come back.

Whenever you leave Scilly (invariably in a state of advanced relaxation bordering on comatose), arriving back in Penzance is a culture shock comparable to being dropped off in south central Los Angeles. But spend a week on an off-island in winter and even getting back to a deserted Hugh Town on St Mary's becomes an intimidating prospect. If Scilly teaches you anything, it's that life is relative.

There's been a lot in the news recently about pubs' newly extended licensing hours, and generally I'm in favour of a more relaxed, continental-style approach. Then again, maybe a tightening-up on opening hours isn't such a bad idea. Say, three hours on a Wednesday night?

Sylvan

2007

I 've never been one for specialist male-interest magazines.
No, not *that* kind; I mean those so-called lads' mags that sit
on coffee tables in Indian takeaways and barbers' throughout
the land. Having little or no interest in football, trendy music,
computer games or pictures of skinny, pampered, teenage
soap-opera actresses in their underwear, I've yet to identify the
publication that meets my exacting requirements.

Cornwall Today, of course, is the closest to what I'd want, but
I have to be honest and say that the day someone publishes a
magazine which regularly features articles on stillwater trout
fishing, choughs, roadster-style motorcycles, Cornwall, Indian
food, traditional British beer, Nigella Lawson, seventies rock
music, exposed-site gardening and chicken/goose husbandry,
well, I'll be first in the queue to take out a lifetime's
subscription. Ah, I can visualise the launch edition now: the
delectable Nigella gazing dreamily from the front cover,
dressed in nothing more than a Cornish Pirates rugby shirt,
prawn jalfrezi all down her front, clasping a pint of Doom Bar
in one hand and a brown trout in the other, with a chough
perched delicately on her head.

In the meantime it's the *West Briton* for me. Risking
accusations of partisanship (it shares, in case you don't know,

its publisher with the very organ you're holding right now), I'd have to say that Thursdays just wouldn't be the same without it. But this has nothing to do with the standard of the journalism therein, nor the fact that the many sections of today's *West Briton* compare so favourably with the meagre broadsheet I remember from my youth. No, it's the property section I'm interested in. Why? Because it's hilarious.

It's the estate agents and their amazing language that fascinates me. These people's command of idiom is inspirational. I have no idea what qualifications you need to become one (you seldom see such jobs advertised), but I reckon to deal confidently in this lingo they must be quite impressive.

Open the paper and examples of their unique art abound. The estate agent doesn't simply describe a house as being 'less than 2 miles from Truro'. Oh no, these besuited wordsmiths flex their semantic muscles by constructing the infinitely more Chaucerian 'Less than two miles *distant* is the historic market town of Truro'. Note '*distant*', instead of '*away*'. And that Truro is not just plain old Truro, with shops and that. Oh no, it's a sort of olde worlde Victorian version of Truro. Truro the *market town*. The words, I presume, are carefully designed to titivate the senses, in order to render the house seeker powerless to resist the charms of the property in question. Another favourite is, '*To* the rear is a large shed' instead of '*At* the rear ...'.

If a house has got trees around it, they like to call it '*sylvan*'. Good Lord, *sylvan*? I don't think I've ever heard someone even *say* 'sylvan', let alone attempt to flog you a house by describing it as such. Maybe I'm mixing with the wrong people. Maybe I need to start hanging out with more Jane Austen readers. And estate agents. I think I might have seen the word *sylvan* in a Ted Hughes poem once, but I can't believe anyone actually talks like that. I'd love to know the estate agents' reason for this odd choice of word. Perhaps they believe that the person lucky enough to buy the house in question will enjoy describing their new home to their friends: "Well, you know, it's really very *sylvan*". At which point their friends would probably be thinking, "Er, do you mean *leafy*?" Where will it end, I ask myself. Will a house on Bodmin Moor be in a *'zephyrous massif location'*? Could an attic sea glimpse become *'an horizonal oceanic belvedere'*?

And then, just as you think you've started to grasp this strange and unfamiliar world of convoluted English, the estate agent turns everything upside down and bowls you a googlie. Suddenly you realise that the barrage of inappropriate adjectives that you've come to love has been chucked out the window in favour of abbreviation. Now it's all *'det 2 bed bung gch, d/g, upvc'*.

Then, for no apparent reason, they switch again and it's back to the flowery stuff. I particularly like the way they say 'Presented to the market with the benefit of central heating', as if it's not at all obvious that having central heating is a benefit. As if there were some circumstances under which central heating would be considered a disadvantage. Perhaps if you'd just moved here from California and weren't up to speed on Cornish domestic heating options. And why do they even need to say, 'Presented to the market'? Isn't that completely obvious, on account of the fact that this is an estate agent's advertisement, and the only function of an estate agent's advertisement is to *present properties to the market*? Next time I sell a car in the *West Briton*, perhaps I'll try something a bit more flowery: *VW Golf, X reg, presented to the market with the benefit of a full service history.*

Quite bizarre. But you've got to love their funny little ways. They get a lot of flak, do estate agents, and I really don't think it's fair. I suggest we all take a step back, look beyond the conventionally held image of the sharp-dressed, sycophantic, money-grabbing estate agent, and appreciate for a moment what a dull world it would be without them.

Flee

2009

W hen I was 18, I couldn't wait to get out of this place. Most of my friends were the same. In fact when I got my first job in a London publishing house after graduating in 1985, I'd regularly bump into beloved Cornish compatriots around the pubs of eighties Covent Garden. *"Right on boy! Comin' fer a pint then or no?"* we'd holler as audibly as possible on spotting one of our tribe coming towards us down Longacre. Like latterday Cousin Jacks, we were making our way in Thatcher's brave new world of, well, publishing, graphic design and advertising. *"Oh, more bloomin' Cornish Mafia,"* my new Londoner friend would say, growing weary of the numbers of incoming young Cornish invading his cosmopolitan home territory.

Twas ever thus. I wasn't the first in my family to leave the comforting bosom of the Cornish Motherland. My grandfather left Truro in the 1920s to seek his fortune in New York. My father went upcountry to do his National Service, then stayed on in Hertfordshire til he'd learned a trade.

But most of us only stay away for a while. This is because most Cornishpersons usually realise pretty sharpish, once they've left, that our quality of life down here is, by and large, a thing to be envied. Of course you can't be expected to know

79

this when you've known nothing else all your life. You've always taken it for granted. Such is the privilege of a Cornish childhood. You assume other places are as good as here.

There's obviously an awful lot to entice your average 20-year-old Cornish boy or girl up to the metropolis. Or abroad. Who can blame Cornish youngsters for seeking exciting bars/events/gigs, interesting people, and the chance to earn considerably more money, in an environment with so many opportunities? Most people living in a geographical extremity will always wonder how things are elsewhere. Call it youthful exuberance, or the early, tentative pangs of wanderlust, but I'd say we should be more worried if today's kids *didn't* want to get out there and see a bit of the world.

So why, then, when they recently interviewed some Truro-based school pupils and discovered that most of them planned to leave the county, was this described as a 'worrying revelation'? As if it were some sort of surprise. Apparently of the 246 interviewees, 46% expressed the desire to work in London, and a lofty 14% were aiming to go to, horror of horrors… *Australia*! The media, in a typically hysterical kneejerk spasm, labelled the phenomenon a 'brain drain', and used the word 'flee' a lot. Surely we don't need to panic about a bit of healthy fleeing, do we?

Well, maybe we do. Things are very different down here these days. The concern is that our kids will go and never come back. It's the great Cornish dichotomy: we've got a university now, and a burgeoning 21st century Cornwall of clued-up, recently graduated 'new media communications consultants' and 'leisure/tourism brand initiation facilitators' is emerging. And these people look very uncomfortable in a Cornwall where unemployed miners sit alongside quota-clogged fisherman chasing dwindling stocks, and the few farms which have escaped being sold off for development are now populated by itinerant foreign labour.

And property prices don't help. Only a handful of years ago Cornwall represented relatively reasonable value for money. But today while we're aware that house prices upcountry have plummeted to Jacobean levels, Cornish ones have dropped to about what they were a week ago Thursday. When all you've got to aim for is a studio flat in a prefabricated timber-framed block, crammed into some weeny, gardenless plot and patronisingly labelled by your struggling local authority as 'affordable' yet still costing more than twice the price of a three bedroom house in Trepiddle ten years ago, well, I'd be considering my fleeing options too.

Perhaps, for once, a bit of media hysteria is justified.

Rambles beyond Railways

2011

T he writer Wilkie Collins is probably best known for *The Woman in White* and *The Moonstone*. Neither of which I've read. But I have just read his 1850 travelogue, *Rambles Beyond Railways*. It's a fascinating account of a walking holiday around Cornwall. The author gets well-immersed in Cornish life, with highlights including a vivid account of descending 420 feet down perpendicular ladders (with broken rungs) into the pitch black, sweaty, working bowels of Botallack mine. He also spends time in a small Cornish fishing village, documenting every person's role in the processing of a million and a half pilchards in a single week. It's a Cornwall we all know existed, but it's captivating to see it brought to life by an eyewitness.

The most notable thing about the book for me, however, was something quite unexpected: the Cornish locals' response when they saw that the author and his companion were travelling on foot. *Out of choice*. They couldn't work it out at all. Most locals thought they were crazy, choosing to travel this way, when they could plainly have afforded one of a range of early Victorian transportation devices to swan about on. Or in. Why, they asked, were they not travelling on horseback? And where was the rest of their stuff? These backpacking ramblers were like aliens in 1850. On arriving at any village, crowds gathered to stare at them with their minimal knapsacks, and speculated as to what on earth they could be doing.

Young Wilkie, brimming with confidence that he's sussed out the best way to see Cornwall, fights his corner with what seems now an evangelical sort of zeal. He's had quite enough of the manifest annoyances of the modern travel age: '...*think of crabbed crossroads, and broken carriage-springs; think of luggage confided to extortionate porters, of horses casting shoes and catching colds...and the next time you leave home, strap your luggage on your shoulders, take your stick in your hand, set forth delivered from a perfect paraphernalia of incumbrances, to go where you will, how you will - the free citizen of the whole travelling world!*' Great stuff, though I'm sure these days we'd all choose a broken carriage spring over a First Great Western replacement bus service anyday. And I've yet to try out his advice on blisters: '...*sponge your feet with cold vinegar and water, change your socks every ten miles, and show me blisters after that, if you can!*'

Obviously 160 years ago a walking holiday on foot represented a far bigger challenge than today. No iPhone app to guide you to the nearest eco-friendly B&B with organic breadmaking facilities. And Wilkie didn't have a pair of light goretex overtrousers to slip on every time the Cornish mizzle turned into Cornish stair rods. He just had to trudge on and try to ignore his moleskin breeches getting heavier and heavier. And imagine the inconvenience of not being able to tweet your friends when you discovered a super, tucked-away gallery with the most divine little limited edition woodcuts. I shudder to think what the Cornish coastline would have been like to navigate without today's handy interpretive signage. I dare say his map was a bit iffy too, especially without one of those waterproof plastic pouches that hangs round your neck to keep it in.

It makes you think. We have so many options for immersing ourselves in Cornwall these days. The visitor can sail it, climb it, cycle it, dive it, camp it, rockpool it, run it, abseil it, surf it, fish it. Oh, and walk it. You can visit moors, estuaries, hills, lakes, coastline, rivers, woods, gardens, pubs, restaurants, museums, galleries, vineyards, nature reserves, breweries, butchers, bakers, candlestick makers. You can see them on foot, in a car, on a yacht, in a plane, on a motorcycle, on a tandem, in a rigid inflatable boat, in a bus, in a hot air balloon.

Yet despite all that, seeing Cornwall on foot is more popular than ever in 2011. As petrol approaches £7 a gallon, Wilkie Collins' sentiments back in 1850 are starting to look quite prophetic.

Opera

2008

T hey were doing it again on the radio the other day.

Some upper class twit droning on about how important it is to have subsidised opera tickets. It's always the same: an out-of-touch arbiter of taste informing us that this most vital of art forms must be preserved, and that it's the moral duty of the musically-enlightened to bring opera 'to the masses'. Regardless of the fact that the masses don't like it very much.

Statistics are always quoted to prove that the masses would simply love to go to the opera, if only the poor misguided dears could stop playing bingo and watching EastEnders long enough. But surely we, the masses, prefer more modern music for the same reason that we prefer a Steven Spielberg film to a Rembrandt portrait. It's a bit more relevant these days. It moves us more. It speaks to us.

Not that I'd ever dream of claiming that there's anything wrong with opera *per se*. If there was, then thousands of people infinitely cleverer than me wouldn't be paying the big bucks to go and experience that awful racket. Oops, there, I said it. I can't stand opera. I think it's dreadful.

This is because I simply don't get it. It doesn't move me on any level: the grotesque facial expressions of the performers, all that bizarre overacting, the peculiar bellowing. I've heard opera fans describe it as a unique blend of art, theatre and music. Well, a lemon curd and marmite sandwich is a unique blend of lemon curd and marmite. That doesn't necessarily make it a good thing.

And why are opera fans so obsessed with volume? If an opera singer can make the other end of an auditorium shake with the frightening and superhuman capacity of their freakishly oversized lungs, they are revered not as a circus act, but as a maestro. Or diva, or whatever. And yet electric amplification has been around for quite some time now. Surely these days we can afford to admit that it's not all about quantity. Personally I'd be happier to listen to the average pub singer doing a Neil Young song than some overweight Italian in a frock going red belting out something written three hundred years ago in a language I don't understand.

But that, really, is a good thing. Art is, by definition, subjective. I don't know why every time I listen to Bruce Springsteen's *Stolen Car* I feel myself welling up (in a good way). I've certainly never stolen a car. It's something very, very deep-seated, and I don't understand it. But I like it. I certainly wouldn't be so pompous as to assume that others should respond in the same way to the same thing, if only they had access to it. I don't care whether anyone else shares my point of view or not. In fact I'm sure most of us don't particularly want others to share our preferences; we want it to be a bit exclusive. We want it to be a personal thing.

That's what gets me about opera. Who has the right to say "This is what we all must listen to, so we must pour thousands of pounds into funding economically unsustainable productions," when people still wouldn't come to see/hear it if it was free every day of the year?

Now, the law of averages dictates that there must be plenty of readers out there who adore opera (fans of opera are absolutely militant about it. More so than any lover of rap music or punk I've come across). So I'd better just point out that in the interests of leading a balanced life I have been to the opera. More than once. I worked in Covent Garden for several years, so felt I had to give it a go in order to improve myself. I was very prepared for it to change my life. I'd have loved that.

But no, after three hours sitting in a sea of sullen faces, all of whom were taking it very seriously indeed (possibly regretfully reflecting on how many times they could have been to see Bruce Springsteen for the same price. Not that many, these days, come to think about it), I still didn't get it.

I suppose I'll just await enlightenment. Sometimes I do hear a little snatch of opera, say, in a film, and think 'that's a lovely tune'. There's that Puccini aria that they used for the football a few years ago. And there are bits of 'light' opera that can be quite catchy. I enjoy having a bash at 'Three little maids from school' when I'm mowing the lawn. You hear nice bits of opera on adverts sometimes. They're only ever thirty seconds long though. It's the other three hours I have a problem with.

Slow

2012

I'm a painfully slow reader. Always have been. How I envied those kids at school who would power through a Wilbur Smith and seemingly recall every detail. I simply couldn't fathom how you could ingest the true meaning of a sentence whilst travelling at such speed. Let alone one sentence after another, page after page. Yet it seemed many of my classmates could. Ern would slam the latest Alistair McLean shut with a satisfied sigh as I sat there struggling to finish the first chapter, and I seriously began to suspect that I was just plain dim. I'd love to be able to say I'd read *Great Expectations* three times by the time I was sixteen, like some people do. But I can't.

My parents even generously paid for me to go on a weekend 'speed reading' course at my school. They did it for all the right reasons, but the course was reprehensible on two counts. Firstly, it took up a weekend, and that meant no skateboarding. Secondly, it was based on a con, because the people running it had cleverly worked out that teenage boys are competitive animals. Thus, after two days of reading practice and eye exercises, every student in the room was keen to prove how fast they had now become. Except for me of course. I hadn't sped up at all, and I was damn well going to stick to my guns. As it was a 'satisfaction or your money back' offer, my folks got their money back. I was the only failure.

Predictably I often took refuge in books with pictures. First, the witty wordplay and wacky illustrations of Dr Seuss. Then, the works of the great Charles Schulz. Courtesy of my Canadian relatives, I was seduced by a perfectly realised world where infants played Beethoven on toy pianos, a dog improbably slept on the roof of his kennel, and a kid clutching a security blanket offered more helpful philosophy than any real life adult. By fourteen I had quite a collection of Peanuts books. I've still got them, and some have probably been read a hundred times.

Charles Schulz once said, '*Winning is great, but it isn't funny. While one person is a happy winner, there may be a hundred losers using funny stories to console themselves*'. If there is a better metaphor for life than Charlie Brown repeatedly running at the football, and Lucy snatching it away at the last minute so that he lands flat on his back, I've yet to come across it. No matter what childhood angst I was having to endure, it was softened by my sharing the travails of perennial loser Charlie Brown. He would have been a slow reader too. He was all I needed.

For years I felt embarrassed that as a teenager I learned more from Schulz than I ever did from Dickens. But now I don't. Now I come across perfectly intelligent people who never spent their youth immersed in *A Christmas Carol* either. I see that my favourite newspaper columnist, Giles Coren, has been a lifelong fan of Goscinny and Uderzo's *Asterix* (admittedly more complex than *Peanuts*, but nevertheless still

89

essentially a cartoon strip). And there are plenty of successful, well-balanced adults who proudly declare that they read nothing but *Marvel* comics as a child. Terry Jones, historian, director, political journalist, not to mention the naked pianist in Monty Python, remains a huge *Tintin* fan. I was actually in rather good company in my preference for books with pictures.

These days I read plenty of books. Proper ones, with no pictures at all. Some of them really long. But it still takes me a while. And I remain deeply suspicious of fast readers. To me they are no different to the hikers I encounter rushing along the coast path, so determined to rack up twenty miles a day that they're afraid to spontaneously stop and look at the view. There's no shame in being a slow reader. I've got to a point where I'm almost proud of it. Charlie Brown's sister Sally said it best: *'I think I've discovered the secret of life - you just hang around until you get used to it'*.

The whale in the cove

2007

B ack in February a dead fin whale was washed up on my
local beach. It was headline news. Most people's natural
reaction was to want to go and see it. Who wouldn't? The fin
whale is the world's second largest whale. I'd seen an
occasional dead dolphin on the beach here before, but this was
the second largest creature on earth, albeit in a bit of a state,
right on our doorstep. Quite an event.

Predictably, we humans immediately sought to take
possession of the situation. The media, keen to find a culprit
for any creature's demise (and unwilling to consider the fact
that wild animals do, just occasionally, die from natural
causes), announced, 'WHALE KILLED BY SHIP' (even though
no-one had yet examined it). And then we, the public, were
warned 'not to approach the animal due to risk of disease and
danger of being cut off by the tide'. This led to sideways
glances as locals were understandably tempted to exploit a
once-in-a-lifetime opportunity to grab a bit of whale for a
souvenir, museum exhibit, or garden feature.

But this whale was on a part of the beach that many locals,
myself included, stroll along all the time when the tide's low. I
wanted a piece of the action. So the next day I walked down
there to take a look, just before sunset.

The tide was only just getting low enough to access the right part of the beach, so people were clambering over rocks to get to the elusive carcass, which was tucked away in the next cove. There was a tangible air of anticipation as I saw people leaving the scene up ahead, all chatting excitedly as they came past me. A couple of characters wearing thick gloves even walked past with a crateful of scavenged whale bits. It seemed the wrecking spirit was still alive and well.

The whale had chosen the most perfect location. It was lying at the base of a colossal cliff, pushed by the tide so far into the cove that it was fully framed on all sides by the most dramatic scenery. Lit by the setting sun, it looked like a stage set. The sensation was that of entering a mausoleum. No-one could say, at this point, if this was to be its final resting place, or whether the tide would yet come and whisk it to another location, but right here and now, it really did seem as if the whale had deliberately picked its own tomb. We just stood in awe, paying our respects to a creature with a bigger brain than us, yet one about which we know so little. This was probably the biggest animal we will see in our lives. I found it comforting that so many people had come.

Almost any other type of creature on earth would have looked insignificant here. But this whale, even in this decomposed state, looked just right. If it was able to command this sort of respect here, now, like this, just imagine what it would have looked like a month ago. I'd have happily carried a rib or a piece of vertebra away with me as a souvenir, but I'm not Superman.

A week later on a crisp, bright, early March day, I popped down to see how what remained of the whale was doing. And it was gone. The cove was just a cove again. The spring tide had obviously been enough to whisk the whole thing back out. I heard that the skin had now washed up half a mile further east. No doubt it had been feeding the fishes all the way there. There had been many discussions about how we humans were going to overcome the problem of vehicular accessibility in order to extricate the seemingly immoveable whale before it decomposed any further.

Thus Nature had scuppered us again. Our clumsy attempts to own the situation were all rendered irrelevant, overnight, by a spring tide, neatly sorting the situation out for us. Our whale was a fleeting moment, a flash in the pan. I hadn't even got a souvenir.

Nature gives us a glimpse of something incredible, and at the same time makes fools of us all.

Babies at Number Ten

2012

R emember what a shock it was when the Blairs had a baby whilst actually in residence at Number Ten? At the time most of us probably thought it was a bit of a one-off. Little Leo was, after all, the first (legitimate) child born to a serving prime minister in over 150 years.

But since then things have changed. Now that the neonatal floodgates have been flung wide open by the Blairs, the first thing on the mind of any incumbent British party leader, let alone PM, these days, seems to be procreation. They're all at it. We Cornish won't forget in a hurry the sight of our newly-elected prime minister standing outside Treliske Hospital a couple of summers ago, announcing the birth of little Endellion (as we struggled to banish from our heads an instantaneous image of a tasty bit of brie).

This was of course lovely for the Camerons, and great that the inspirational staff at Treliske hospital got a bit of positive publicity for a change. And then what did Ed Miliband do, mere weeks after being elected leader of the Labour party? Yep, introduced us to little Samuel.

So what's it all about? Is it simply that parents these days feel they can choose to have a family later, and party leaders are no different? Or are party leaders just getting younger?

Let's be honest. Wouldn't we all be more comfortable if prime ministers looked a bit more like Stanley Baldwin and a bit less like Dave Cameron being all touchy-feely and kicking back on Polzeath beach in head to toe Boden? Safe pair of hands and all that. I never wanted to hear Tony Blair playing that guitar he was so famously spotted carrying into Number Ten. I really wasn't interested in that side of him. It wasn't as if I'd ever have bought his album. I'd prefer it if the prime minister was too busy running the country. As for infants' screams echoing down the hallowed halls of Number Ten, not on Winston Churchill's watch there weren't. You can't imagine Lloyd George interrupting his war cabinet to consult a well-thumbed copy of Gina Ford's *Potty Training in One Week*. Well, actually maybe you could. Apparently his loins were still fruitful at 66. Bad example.

I remember when Nick Clegg, our deputy leader, was on *Desert Island Discs* the very week that the government began announcing the details of the most drastic cuts in a generation. "You look very tired if you don't mind me saying so," said Kirsty Young. And what did he blame for his tiredness? After mentioning the fact that he'd had to make a lot of tough choices, his equally relevant reason was apparently the fact that he had three young children.

Now that really isn't right, is it? I know as well as anyone that looking after children is an extremely important job, but surely you have to review your workload when you've signed up for running the country. I mean, running the country is really, *really* important. As important as it gets. It's OK to blame your kids' sleeping habits for your bleary eyes if you're a nobody like me. But running the country is not the same. As far as I'm concerned it's just fine for all other people in Britain to have such concerns. But not the PM. Or the deputy one. You want somebody who can concentrate on the national good. Somebody who spends absolutely no time whatsoever fretting over whether or not little Jonty has had his Calpol.

I'm not buying it anyway. Keen as they may be to insinuate that they are normal just like us, the fact is that your average prime minister tends to have a considerable amount of backup. Speaking as a parent of twin four-year-olds who doesn't, I feel compelled to point out rather bitterly that there's just no way these people are going to be up at 3am scraping sick off the carpet. One has, you know, *staff* for these sorts of things.

Anticipation

2009

I t's that time of year again: the season of anticipation. A particularly vile winter has coughed its last few drizzly breaths, and we really can start to look forward to those long summer days.

First the daffodils and primroses splattered the hedgerows with the bright promise of spring, and now it's the turn of the bluebells and wild garlic. Then it'll be magenta time, as the red campion and valerian mingle with towering foxgloves and cheeky whistling jacks, while the cow parsley's tightly packed flowerheads wait impatiently in the wings.

Meanwhile the birds grow frantic in their life and death struggle to renew their species at any cost. The blackbird's impossibly beautiful song becomes the first thing we hear in the morning and about the last thing we hear in the evening.

We think about turning the Rayburn off for the summer, we dust off last year's shorts and see just how tight the waistband has become after a long winter's comfort eating, and we pray that the mower will start, despite the fact that we never got round to having it serviced this winter. Again. A spirit of optimism envelops us at this time of year, for however bad the previous summer's weather was, we always anticipate the summer of '76. It's the triumph of hope over experience.

And paradoxically it's the only time of year when there's anything worth watching on the telly. First there's the fresh thrill of this year's *Chelsea Flower Show*, with all its ludicrous yet compelling excesses. Then, it being spring, a young man's thoughts turn to Kate Humble. We begin three weeks of *Springwatch*, and ironically I always end up videoing it on account of the fact that it's spring and you don't want to be stuck inside watching TV. After all, you've got the real thing happening live all around you in the garden.

Then as Mr Oddie removes his foot from his mouth and scuttles back to London, and the 500,000 miles of cable on that farm are coiled up until next year, you still can't turn the telly off as the British national sport of *Wimbledon* is about to start.

But then you get to the other side of *Wimbledon*, and things don't look so bright. Suddenly, out of nowhere, it's midsummer, and you've had the longest day already. Why does it come so soon? Will I forever go through life thinking the longest day must be sometime in August, like it was when I was young? You're into late June and now you drive to the beach and get stuck behind a people carrier with a vast pod on top that somehow prevents it from exceeding twenty miles per hour. When you get there, you find the National Trust have put up the parking by yet another pound.

Back home in the garden those spring daffodils have become spent ribbons of khaki slime strewn in amongst all the perennials, preventing you from getting at the weeds properly and making everything look a right mess. On TV, three weeks of *Springwatch* four times a week have turned into three months of *Big Brother* twenty four hours a day. And the magical, optimistic blackbird-filled evenings of May are replaced by evenings in which we pay the price for living on the coast road. Our ears struggle to cope with a mad parade of deafening vehicles, all clammering to drive as quickly as humanly possible if the sun's out, and all wanting to share the good news with the rest of the world in the form of decibels. And you know that by September you'll never remember the names of the players you actually cared about at *Wimbledon*, just as you'll have forgotten the names of the animals on *Springwatch*.

But it's all right. This summer everything's going to be different. This summer we've got nothing to worry about, because I overheard someone down the pub saying it's going to be a hot one. Hotter than '76, apparently.

Bitter and twisted

2007

I couldn't help noticing in last month's *Cornwall Today* a letter in which 'a bitter and twisted old Cornishman' complained that the magazine targets 'yuppie Steinites and people retiring to Cornwall'. In particular, he expressed concern about families moving down here and 'how nice they think it is'. I expect one of the red rags to this Cornish bull was a feature in the previous month's issue, in which the most recent London arrivals in a Cornish village stated, bold as you like, that 'some of our best friends are going to move down in the next two years'. I could sense property prices oscillating upwards in that particular village.

I'm really not sure who to sympathise with. Any Cornish person's hackles must have bristled uncontrollably on reading such flagrant insensitivity to the plight of young Cornish locals, the vast majority of whom are growing up in a Cornwall where they have precious little chance of ever owning their own home. I know loads of them. Yet it's a free country, and who in their right mind wouldn't move here, especially when you listen to constant news items about rising crime levels upcountry, traffic congestion and so on. Then there's our milder climate, world class scenery, a more relaxed attitude, the beaches, the lack of cities. So it seems a bit harsh to blame the incomers and the holiday home-owners individually for this fairly recent phenomenon.

Us Cornish have, when you think about it, a lot in common with these people. They simply want to introduce into their lives an experience that we have always had. They were just a bit late cottoning on. And anyway, people have always been drawn here. Cornwall is richer for it as a result. Daphne du Maurier, Rick Stein, Alfred Wallis, Tim Smit. All incomers. Strewth, I married one myself.

Sometimes I feel that all us Cornish want is a bit of respect. Perhaps this is really what got Mr Bitter and Twisted Old Cornishman's goat. It's the arrogant assumption by some incomers that Cornwall is a sort of idyllic holiday camp where you can lead some self-conceived idea of a hedonistic, alternative lifestyle. A theme park that's there purely for their own self-indulgent pleasure. Our history and culture is largely overlooked.

Then if it doesn't measure up to their expectations, they complain. I really cannot stand hearing people who, having moved down here for the 'lifestyle', whine about some aspect of life in Cornwall being too provincial. If you can't get a decent macchiato, or a shop's shut early, rejoice! You're getting the real Cornwall! That's the whole point! You can't have your cherry truffle torte and eat it. Come on, if you want a cup of the latest steam-injected coffee trend, go to Covent Garden. If you want the freshest piece of fish you've ever eaten, or a real pasty, or some cream that you can stand your spoon up in, go to Cornwall.

People who complain about Cornwall being provincial need to bear in mind that the place has changed beyond recognition already. It wasn't long ago you couldn't move for Land Rovers and muck in Truro on a Wednesday morning, when farmers came from miles around to buy and sell, right in the middle of town. And you wouldn't find a shop open on a Thursday afternoon. And you had to go to Falmouth if you wanted the unalloyed pleasure of the Marks and Spencers retail experience. Oh yes, things have changed a lot just recently. I'm nervous that if they change much more, we really won't recognise the place as Cornwall at all.

It's been a long time coming, this sudden influx of people who appreciate what a great place this is to live. And I can't see any obvious solution to the property paradox it's created. At the risk of patronising Mr Bitter and Twisted Old Cornishman in the face of what he seems to consider an alien invasion, the only solace I can offer is to count his blessings. Considerable pleasure can be derived from watching the over-enthusiastic habits of the incoming retired, desperate to embrace their new sub-tropical lifestyle by wearing shorts all year round, their skin burnt to a scarlet leathery crisp by mid-May due to endless back garden sun worship. Likewise the smug fat cat 'urban surfers', down for the weekend in their City bonus-financed holiday home, unwittingly standing out like a sore thumb in their too-shiny car, with their too-new surfboard, clad from head to foot in way too many surf labels.

Mr Bitter and Twisted Old Cornishman, your kids may never afford a home of their own, every house in your street

102

may stand empty for forty-eight weeks of the year, and you may no longer recognise your village as the butchers and newsagents are replaced by the art galleries and bars. But hey, at least you can relish the fact that you were here first.

Water

2007

I need something explaining. Recently I was in a large supermarket, minding my own business. Suddenly I realised I was in an entire department which sold only one product. The odd thing was that this stuff was the one item in the shop that is, by definition, free. There were weeny bottles of it on shrink-wrapped cardboard trays, and great flagons, and every size in between. Some fizzy, some still. Some infused with 'a hint of' some fruity flavour, rather like that paint that everyone slapped around their living rooms in the eighties which was basically white with a virtually undetectable colour in it. There was funky sports packaging, and there was sophisticated foreign packaging. There were countless different makes, some bottled in Britain, some imported from the other side of the world. Every taste was catered for, every demographic pandered to. When I counted them, there were over seventy ways to purchase water.

This is a very surreal situation, isn't it? Here we are, living in a country privileged enough to have perfectly good drinking water coming out of our taps, while over a billion people in the world have no access to drinkable water. Yet instead of rejoicing, and counting our blessings, we're flocking to the shops to buy the stuff in bottles. Have I missed something?

Does water in bottles not often cost more than petrol, or milk, and is it not thousands of times more expensive than what comes out of the tap, even taking into account the price of tap water in Cornwall?

Yes, apparently in Britain last year we gaily spent £2 billion on bottles of something that falls from the sky. It seems many people's taste buds are so finely tuned these days that the very idea of drinking common old water from the tap has become unthinkable. Why? Well, when I've asked people to explain their resolute avoidance of tap water, it's amazing the stuff they come out with. Revulsion at the thought of the chlorine in it, fear of the lead, or of the flouride. And yet last year tap water in 99.96% of 4.5 million homes tested apparently met standards set by European and UK drinking water regulations.

I read the other day that if you let it sit for half and hour, the chlorine in tap water evaporates anyway. I know that in our house we've taken to putting a jug of it in the fridge, and it tastes great. Or rather, it tastes of absolutely nothing, which I guess is what you're after with water. Whether it's the cold temperature (which, let's face it, removes the flavour from most things), or the evaporation of the chlorine, I defy anyone to tell the difference between Cornish tap water from my fridge and posh bottled water. And yet why, when I'm in a restaurant, do I always feel so cheap asking for tap water?

I suppose the sad reality is that I'm just not that sophisticated. I simply don't have the refined palette required to detect the difference between chilled tap water and poncy bottled water. Perhaps someone could start up a weekend course to teach you such things. It could be along the lines of those fine wine appreciation classes. More complicated obviously, as telling the difference between different sorts of water is surely a far more finite business than it is with wine, which comes in all sorts of different colours.

I find this weird revolution peculiar on so many levels. But it's the packaging I object to more than anything. Regardless of how recyclable all these millions of plastic bottles are, if we didn't buy them, we wouldn't need to recycle them at all. Deep down I suspect buying bottled water has actually got more to do with being seen to be drinking it, as it's indicative of a certain affluence, like a designer pair of jeans.

But hey, it's a free country. And fair enough, I've got friends who swear that the tap water in their house is so chlorinated that you can smell it in a cup of coffee from across the kitchen. Which is, granted, pretty bad. Maybe one day I'll join all those decadent spurners of tap water. Just as soon as I've completely removed from my diet all the poisonous, processed ready meals, steroid-fattened, factory-farmed meat, chemical-laden fizzy drinks, and all the E numbers in all the crisps, and snacks, and biscuits. When I can run ten miles a day, avoid ever passively inhaling a breath of someone's cigarette, or a cubic centimetre of carbon monoxide from a passing car exhaust, then, and only then, will I be pure enough to need bottled water.

Kernow King

2011

I met someone the other day who'd never heard of the Kernow King. I know. It seems incredible to me too. But it then occurred to me that there might be others, so I thought I'd give him a quick mention. I actually think he might be more important than we realise.

The Kernow King is a comedy character created by Cornishman Edward Rowe. I became a fan about a year ago, when I saw a link on Facebook (oh yes, it has its uses). Basically he makes funny little videos and puts them on *YouTube*. Subjects range from a *'Who killed Mavis Davis?'* whodunit, to a *'Day off in Looe'* (geddit?) spoof public information film, to my personal favourite, *'Pasty die(t)'*. I should point out that he occasionally alludes to more adult themes that we won't go into here for reasons of modesty and the fact that you may be reading this before the watershed.

The films don't exactly look scripted (well, not in any obvious way), and they can meander all over the place. But my goodness, are they funny. With the aid of his friend Simon Bugler, clearly a capable filmmaker, producer and editor, the Kernow King is a fully-developed, loveable comedy character. He's charming. He ticks all the boxes, including his very adept use of a number of excellent catchphrases (...*Live in*

Cornwall…Work the jacket….). Of course it does him no harm at all that he's actually a pleasant-looking chap (my wife tells me). Once you've watched him a couple of times, he doesn't even have to say that much. You just look at him, and smile. As the King himself would say, "'e's some bleddy boy".

As a result, the Kernow King has become something of a cult phenomenon. Early last year his bleak Cornish version of a sun-drenched California tourist board promotional video won first prize in a competition. He now has thousands of followers interacting with him daily on his Facebook page. His success has been, er, viral, I think it's called.

Now I spend a lot of time fretting about us Cornish becoming so inconsequential in our own county/country that we're becoming an insignificant, beleaguered minority. For some, the answer is to breathe a bit of life back into our moribund language. But I think the Kernow King is doing something just as significant. He's luxuriating in his Cornishness, and his audience is joining in. But we're so busy chuckling at his antics that we barely notice. And when you're laughing, you're taking it in without thinking about it. You don't have to attend evening classes. When he hilariously goes on his experimental month-long pasty diet and gazes adoringly upon his final pasty the day before his exclusively pasty diet begins, it's a great joke. Sure, he's playing the affable buffoon, but he's reaching a huge audience and flying the flag at the same time.

I had no idea there were that many young people out there revelling in being Cornish (I didn't think that many people cared any more), but I'm thrilled to see there are. I've waffled on before on this page how important I think it is that we don't lose touch with day-to-day words and expressions. No-one can remember how to say, "How you goin' on boy?" in the original Cornish language, but if we ever forget to say it at all, then we really have lost our Cornish soul.

Of course, like any cult thing, I've got mixed feelings about mentioning this out loud, because I don't know how I feel about the Kernow King ever becoming 'mainstream'. But hang, he deserves it. He's put the hours in. It may well not be your thing anyway; he can be a bit fruity at times.

All right, I've said me bit. Cheers and gone.

Grey

2007

On a recent trip upcountry my wife and I spent some time discussing what a large proportion of cars on the road seem to be grey. So as we embarked on the homeward journey we conducted a little survey to pass the time. One of us counted all the cars coming the other way, and the other counted how many of them were grey. The result was amazing. 40% of the first two hundred cars coming the other way were various shades of grey.

Why? What does this say about people? Why is this colour so incredibly popular (actually is it even a colour, containing no pigment)? I'm no expert, but I'm sure that with recent advances in paint technology the range of beautiful colours and finishes must be quite limitless. If they can guarantee your car against corrosion for ten years, I'll bet they can magic up absolutely any colour you like. Yet we constantly buy cars that look like they forgot to paint them. Is grey not exactly the colour that the thing started out as in the first place, in its raw state? The colour of bare, unadorned metal?

Now of course the statistics make it inevitable that I would know several grey car owners (the car, not the owner), and indeed this is true. So I asked them why they made this most tedious of choices. The only consistent answer I got was that "it looks really classy". *Classy?* Have I missed something? A grey car doesn't say 'classy' to me. It says, "I couldn't make my mind up, so I opted for the colour that's not even a colour". The very word is used to denote dullness and vagueness. Grey area, grey sky, grey hair, grey pants. It is, truly, the John Major of colours. I wouldn't call any type of grey desirable.

Personally I'm unlikely to ever be faced with such a dilemma myself, as I'm not the sort of chap who will ever buy a new car. But I do worry that there's quite a high probability that next time I go to buy a used car, the perfect one might happen to be grey. I mean, the market's going to be flooded with them. I imagine the conversation might go something along the lines of:

Me: "And how much are you prepared to knock off due to the fact that they forgot to send it to the paint shop?"

Vendor: "Uh? But it looks classy."

With an alizarin crimson car, or an ultramarine car I'd definitely feel I was getting a bit more for my money (I wouldn't want a green car though. Everyone knows they're unlucky).

As usual I think I must be missing something. 40% of car drivers is a pretty significant number. Practically a majority. Yet it's not as if we seek out greyness in other areas of our lives. Every few weeks the Sunday supplements are instructing us which new colour is 'in' for that month. If you're looking for a jacket that is. But with cars it's a lot more subtle. It seems that although we want to stand out from the crowd, keep up with the Joneses, and assert that we're different to the others, the urge to declare our individualism extends no further than the daring decision to choose a grey car which is slightly greeny-looking, or a grey car with just the tiniest hint of blue. For the even less adventurous there's *dark* grey, which I'd call pale black, or light metallic grey that I've heard described as silver. Silver being pale, shiny grey.

It's such a shame. It's not as if we need things any greyer on our grey little island. Perhaps that's it. Subliminally people think a grey car fits in here, because it matches the weather, and our overtaxed, overcrowded, grey mood. I have to say from a safety perspective a camouflaged car probably isn't a particularly sensible option though. Put it this way: I doubt grey cars are this popular in Jamaica. And I don't think they look right in Cornwall either, where the sun always shines and life is good, or so we like to think. You wouldn't want a beach buggy in grey, now would you?

But now there's hope. I read recently that after enjoying its status as Britain's most popular colour for several years, grey / silver is on its way out, and falling in the rankings. Seems we've literally seen the light, and are returning to a more enlightened age when we appreciated our ability to embrace colours. I got quite excited when I read that there's a new colour in town, one that's already overtaken the popularity of grey. Thank goodness, I thought. Until I realised what the colour was.

Black. Lord help us all.

Brown signs

2005

D riven anywhere in the Cornish countryside lately? Noticed anything? It seems as you approach any junction and scan the signpost for the whereabouts of the village you're aiming for, you find yourself bombarded by a rapidly increasing barrage of information about places you don't want to go. All attractively presented on pseudo-rural-looking, tasteful brown signs.

One particular Cornish pub springs to mind. Situated right on the river, it has to be approached down several miles of leafy lanes (assuming you're not blessed with a boat of course). The very act of finding the place used to be an experience in itself, part of the entertainment, part of the reason you went there. "Ah, now, how did we get there last time?" you'd say. "Was it two lefts and then a right, or two rights and then a left? Did we go straight across at the big oak tree?" The only clue they gave you was a small wooden sign nailed to a tree at one particularly tricky junction, presumably placed there many years before by some long-forgotten landlord, and now virtually smothered by ivy (the sign, not the landlord, obviously). Admittedly a small, ivy-clad sign isn't that useful unless you happen to know where to look for it, but my point is that it was all part of the experience. You felt like you were at that hard to find, out-in-the-middle-of-nowhere pub before you even arrived at it. When you did get there, well, you were Dr Livingstone arriving at Victoria Falls. It was great. You'd made it. You'd earned your pint of HSD or crab sandwich. Or trip to the toilet.

But now, in this 2005 version of the Cornish rural experience, how do we approach the same pub? Well, the first thing we see is a stupid brown sign, there on the main road, telling you to turn off. Then as soon as there's any risk that you might take another turning and go in the wrong direction, there's another horrible great brown sign to keep you on track. And more, bold as you like, at every junction, every place you could conceivably take a wrong turn. By the time you get to the pub you might as well be arriving at bloody Ikea. All the fun's gone out of it. It's become a joyless, heartless experience.

There are now no less than four brown signs on the junction nearest my house, all advertising places which I'm sure 99% of passers-by already know are there. What's it all about? Call me old-fashioned, but I liked it when you had to search out a place you wanted to go to using directions, a map and perhaps the odd hand-painted sign nailed to a post. I liked having to exercise my sense of direction once in a while. Or at least my wife's, which is far better than mine. These blots on the landscape are turning Cornwall into some weird 21st century pastiche of itself as a rural idyll. And being brown isn't fooling anyone.

Obviously most businesses would probably say, 'But brown signs are good for trade'. I'm sure plenty of them are. And being relatively inexpensive to buy, I suppose it makes sense to get one. All I'm saying is, there's a time and a place. Things have got out of hand. This is Cornwall. I'm not sure how we compare with other counties with our proliferation of brown signs, but surely we must have more than most. There are many, many places for people to visit here. Pubs, gardens, buildings, restaurants, tourist attractions of all types, for all types of people. Selling a brown sign to every American burger bar, go-cart track or tacky tourist stall that wants one is really starting to devalue the more appropriate applicants.

I suppose it's always possible that it doesn't really matter. Maybe we should all just sit back while Cornwall turns into an increasingly sanitised, generic theme park, with a rapidly dwindling sense of discovery, and everything carefully laid out in front of us, neatly labelled. After all, I'm sure we've all been to the odd restaurant or bar where they've done such a convincing job turning a modern concrete building into an authentic Mexican taverna that by the time you've had a couple of tequilas you've completely forgotten how you got there, and you'd swear you were in a stinking back alley in Tijuana. But I don't think so. Not in Cornwall. I'm not taking it. I won't be going back to that Cornish pub until the management has seriously reconsidered its signage. When I next meander down that lane, I want to stand at least a 70% chance of getting hopelessly lost. It's the whole point.

Mundic

2013

Yesterday I was driving down a little lane that I don't use very often. Two friends of mine happen to live along there, and I hadn't seen them for a while, so I told myself that if their car was outside, I'd pop in and say hello. Sure enough their car was there. But their house wasn't.

As I walked up the path it became obvious that their plan to scat their mundic bungalow down and build something nicer in its place had advanced more quickly than I'd realised. The roof was gone, and the walls were reduced to huge piles of mundic block fragments. Mundic block, in case you don't already know, was a building material used to build thousands of properties in Cornwall during the first half of the twentieth century. The blocks were made from mine waste mixed with cement, and were presumably super cheap. But it turned out not to be such a great idea when people began to notice that when damp got to the concrete, it started to crumble. Not a good thing in a house. Anyone buying a Cornish property of a certain age these days gets a mundic test done. Depending on the grade of mundic it can be fine, but it can be a bit of a minefield. If you're ever house-hunting on *Rightmove*, and you come across a house that looks suspiciously good value, chances are as you read through the estate agent's seductive blurb, you'll eventually reach the words, 'Cash purchasers only'. The fact is that mundic, even good mundic, makes us all uncomfortable. Especially those handing out mortgages.

It's not all bad news though. Mundic houses can be a bit of a bargain for those with cash upfront. And of course a mundic house in a desirable location provides developers with a golden opportunity. Thus all over Cornwall you see rather nice houses popping up in the place of old mundic ones as people maximise their site.

My friends down the lane were actually rather attached to their mundic bungalow, and celebrated its dodgy credentials by renaming it affectionately as 'Mundique'. But the time had come to replace it with something modern and eco-friendly and beautiful. As we stood there among the piles of rubble they said, "D'you want a bit of mundic to take away with you? Sort of like a souvenir?" They were joking, of course, but I took the opportunity to pick up a brick-sized fragment and turn it over in my hands. I realised I'd never seen an actual mundic block before. It looked like a piece of ordinary breeze block, but with big chunks of randomly shaped aggregate in it, and browner in colour. I assumed it would crumble easily in my hands, but it didn't. I thought about my very old cottage, and wondered whether its cob and shale and bits of eighteenth century spittle, hair and feathers are really all that preferable to mundic.

I actually liked the idea of taking a bit of mundic away with me, maybe to display in the front porch, as a curio to show people. But a strange fear came over me. The same fear I experience whenever I consider bringing a cutting of Japanese knotweed home to grow in a pot. It is, after all, a beautiful plant. But then I always remember those horror stories about people inadvertently introducing a morsel of knotweed stuck to the sole of their shoe, and a year later it's taken over the whole garden, eaten the driveway, and kidnapped one of the children. I knew it was ridiculous, and yet somewhere deep inside me I sensed that to deliberately bring a piece of mundic block onto my property could have similar repercussions, infecting my house, and contaminating all in its wake.

I threw it back on the rubble pile. And noticed, as it landed, that it cracked in half.

Polytunnel

2007

I 've got a bit of land out the back. You might almost call it a
paddock. And I've always wanted a greenhouse, but never
got round to installing one. So a couple of years ago, when a
friend said he was getting rid of an old thirty-by-eighteen foot
polytunnel, well, it seemed fate had taken a hand.

Being a rather lazy gardener, I presumed that this structure
would be the answer to any horticultural problem I'd ever had.
I could grow stuff to eat, and propagate ornamental plants to
my heart's content. I started dreaming about a brave new
thermoplastic world bursting with healthy, succulent
'*Schwartzkopf*' aeoniums which I would then sell on for
surprising profits. It was to be a utopian world where
tomatoes, broad beans and aubergines would rub shoulders
with semi-ripe hebe cuttings (well, not rub shoulders *literally*,
for that would be shabby horticultural practice, and an
invitation for botrytis and downy mildew).

I couldn't wait. Sensibly, I helped my friend Stuart dis-
mantle his vast metal hoops (he was replacing his polytunnel
with a bigger, posher one), and even took photos of each joint
for the record. I couldn't lose. "It'll be fine," says Stuart, who is
six foot something, ex-navy and built like a brick outhouse.
He's one of those 'Can do' types, the type that 'Rather not do'

types like me find so inspiring. "I'll come over and help you put it up when the time comes," he said, looking convincingly into my eyes and simultaneously whacking seven bells out of a reluctant, rusted-up metal joint.

Now I admit that one of my main frames of reference in the world of polytunnels is *The Archers*, when Adam persuaded Brian Aldridge that they needed to invest in a number of them to get the new strawberry venture up and running. Radio drama being what it is, one minute they were talking about it, the next they were packing the strawberries off to farmers' markets all over Borsetshire. It was so easy. The same could not be said of my own erection.

A polytunnel might just look like a line of hoops with plastic on them. It did to me anyway. And that's not surprising, because when you look at it from the outside that's all you see. When you go inside one, you're too busy looking at all the lovely plants to notice how it's put together. But I can tell you, there's more to it than meets the eye. Obviously if I'd simply bought a new polytunnel, with instructions and no missing bits, things would have been considerably easier. But that's not really my style, on account of my dedication to the principle of recycling. That and my enthusiasm to do it all on the cheap.

So I took delivery of the pickup load of rusty steel poles in varying stages of dilapidation, and embarked on several months of sourcing missing spigots and ferrules. After an afternoon spent wandering around the scrapyard at Macsalvors, forlornly searching for the right gauge steel tubing, I persuaded a mechanic friend to weld some new brackets. I sourced suppliers of bolts and anti-hotspot tape (prevents friction between the new plastic sheet and the tubes you see). It was hard for me. I'm no engineer. My brother was the one with the Meccano set. I was more of a 'throw your Action Man parachutist out of the bathroom window and chuck stones at him as he descends' kind of kid.

I then mixed huge amounts of cement to bed the poles into the ground properly, industriously employing the spirit level at every possible juncture to ensure everything was perfectly straight. I was sustained by visions of a new horticultural empire looming. It was to be my Field of Dreams, for surely, if I built it, they would grow.

After ten months of fiddling about, and two-and-a-half cans of WD-40, the vast hoops were in position, the wooden raised beds had been constructed, and weed-suppressing black sheeting was pegged down to the entire floor area. A deep trench had been dug ready for the plastic, door frames installed, and a huge roll of plastic sheeting was standing by, waiting for its moment of glory. All we needed now was a calm day. A really calm day, because if you've ever tried holding a sixty-foot sheet of heavy polythene in the air in anything more than a very light breeze, you'll know that it's not the sort of thing you want to be doing very often, unless you're trying to invent a new extreme sport. Three times Stuart and I arranged to do it, and three times we had to cancel, due to it being a bit blowy. I was seriously starting to think it might never happen.

But the fourth time we were lucky. We didn't take off once. An amazing metamorphosis occurred within a couple of hours. The thing went from looking like an embarrassing bit of rusty old abandoned scaffolding to a bona fide horticultural structure. It looked rather beautiful, actually – translucent white, tight as a drum (mostly) and immaculately clean. "Don't they look lovely, when they're new?" observed Stuart, rather inviting the question, "Why, what will it look like in a year's time?"

So what happened then? Was it the answer to all my problems? Did things grow? Oh yes. Things were to get pretty interesting.

Tap washers
v Surfboards

2010

I n 1946, the grandfather of a friend of mine bought an ironmongers shop in Perranporth. It was right across the road from that fabulous beach. Then in 1977, his son persuaded him to turn one side of the shop into a surf shop, selling wetsuits, boards and wax. It became, I have to say, a mightily cool place to hang out when I was eighteen. The ironmongery still sustained the business during the winter months by supplying locals with fish hooks, nuts, bolts and tap washers. The arrangement worked, for a while. But the writing was on the wall. In 1988, father and son made the painful but realistic decision to remove the ironmongery altogether. Now it was a bona-fide surf shop. They'd seen the future, and they were right.

Nothing is more central to the metamorphosis that's recently happened in Cornwall than the rise and rise in the popularity of surfing. Sure, there will be plenty of sunburned wannabes and hangers on at this year's *Boardmasters* in Newquay, but there will also be thousands and thousands of people who surf. Really surf. Thirty years ago you never saw a car heading west on the A30 with a surfboard on the roof. It

123

would have looked odd. Nowadays people wouldn't drive to Cornwall without one. We all know surfing brings millions into the Cornish economy every year. The waves might be an awful lot more crowded these days, but as far as Cornwall's concerned, this is a good thing.

The *Boardmasters* surf event has actually been going since 1983. I used to go to it back then, and it was a far cry from the five day 'Surf, skate and music festival' it is today. That first year it was called the *Foster's Europro,* as I recall. The first day I visited, the Radio One roadshow was happening in the car park at Fistral at the same time. All the holidaymakers (that's what we called them then) jostled for a glimpse of DJ Dave Lee Travis, while, a few yards away on the beach, a modest crowd of local surfers gathered around some ramshackle awnings to watch pro surfers competing in heats. And those pro surfers, well, they were gods.

It's not too strong a word to use. As a Cornish teenager in the seventies, my heroes weren't footballers or actors. They were Californian skateboarders and Australian surfers. It was their names and their sponsors I doodled on my schoolbooks. These were people I'd only ever dreamt of seeing in a magazine, or in a rarely screened surf movie. So imagine our excitement when our gods came calling.

In 1983, on Fistral beach, I had a chat with Tom Carroll. I really did. I was nervous, awestruck, overwhelmed. But he was just sitting there, and he noticed me taking a picture of him, and we started talking. Who's Tom Carroll? In 1983 he was Usain Bolt. He was Roger Federer. Or, if you're a surfer, he was a young Kelly Slater. Carroll won the world title that year, and the year after. And there he was, sitting under an awning on Fistral beach. And it wasn't just Tom Carroll at Fistral. Next to him was four times World title runner up Aussie Cheyne Horan. Then there was legendary veteran ex-world champion Shaun Tomson. Oh, and Rabbit Bartholomew, who was, and I'm quite sure will always be, the most stylish man I have ever seen ride a wave.

Here they were, these living legends, and they were being ignored by most people. I couldn't believe it. But that was 1983. Everything's changed now. Today's pro surf gods are given the attention they deserve. And even if Radio One did co-book the Fistral site for their roadshow (or whatever it's called nowadays), I'm quite sure the crowd would happily flit between the two. The Facebook generation mixes it up, moving comfortably between all kinds of worlds. Worlds that previously seemed completely incompatible.

One thing's for sure. Surfing's here to stay. My friend's dad's surf shop, now in new hands, is still thriving. And there are four others now on the same street.

Camping

2005

My wife and I just got back from a bit of camping on Exmoor. Lovely it was. But admitting to people that you're partial to camping can be a perplexing experience. When I mention it, you'd be surprised how often people say something along the lines of, "What? You *camped*?!" as if it was some disgraceful clandestine perversion I was admitting to.

OK, we *were* in Devon, but apart from that it was all perfectly above board.* Part of you wants to shout back at them, explaining that there's nothing to touch it, remembering the people you've met camping over the years, and the places you've been as a result of the flexibility it gives you, and the life-changing experiences it's led to. Experiences you certainly wouldn't get in some posh hotel. But then there's a part of you that thinks no, why let them in on the secret? Everyone might catch onto it, and then where would we be?

I think we've become conditioned to assuming that luxury is preferable to experience. When a competition prize is declared 'The dream holiday of a lifetime!' it usually features accommodation in some swanky five star hotel. Why? I don't get it. If you were staying in a stunning, exotic part of the world, experiencing cultures and scenery you'd previously only dreamed of, why would you choose to dine surrounded by bored businessmen and fat millionaires who don't know any better, with whom you have nothing in common? You'd feel obliged to never leave the hotel, just to maximise the facilities. Give me a tent any day.

Camping in this country seems to be stigmatised by many as little more than:

a) a losing battle against inclement weather.

b) a holiday for those who can't afford one involving four walls and a roof.

Well, to tackle these point by point, a) As the old saying goes, 'There's no such thing as bad weather, only inappropriate clothing'. Prepare for bad weather, and take measures to ensure that your tent doesn't leak (for the leaking tent is truly a woeful thing), and get on with it.

As for b), the fact that people in our status-obsessed society can only associate camping with poverty, well, they really have missed the point. I know loads of people who could easily afford a hotel and choose to camp. The bonus is that the money they're saving on unnecessary luxury can be more usefully spent on more interesting pursuits. Ones that they'll remember. No-one ever lay on their death bed saying "Ah, do you remember the time we stayed at the Umbongo Regal? What about the quality of that bedroom carpet? And how delightfully servile all the staff were?" I don't think so. Perhaps some people feel the need to have an expensive-looking holiday as some sort of status symbol. But I don't think perceived wealth is quite what it used to be. Being seen spending lots of money doesn't necessarily impress people like it once did. Thanks to our modern credit culture, the days are gone when you could judge a person's wealth by the quality of their possessions. Nowadays the age and size of a car more often reflects the level of debt a person is willing to take on in a misguided attempt to impress passers-by.

Camping doesn't even have to be cheap. You can spend an awful lot of money and still, technically, be camping. In Canada we travelled with a family whose 'recreational vehicle' was so vast it featured a full-size three piece suite and a TV in every room. But then at the other end of the scale in Zambia we once picked up an Australian hitchhiker who'd pretty much gone native. He carried a small saucepan, a tiny bivouac tent, a blanket, a bottle of antiseptic for his foot infection, and a passport. It all fitted into a bag smaller than your average pillowcase. He was one of the happiest people I've ever met.

But be warned: camping is addictive. The more you do, the more you crave it. My wife and I dread walking into our village during the summer because there's a lovely campsite down the road. We find ourselves peering enviously over the hedge at the happy campers, all comfortable in the knowledge that they're just that little bit closer to nature, knowing that there's no need to ring room service for an alarm call, because the dawn chorus will take care of it. We see their day's damp towels drying on makeshift clothes lines, and we breathe in the variety of cooking smells wafting through the warm evening air. We sigh and lament the fact that we can't join them. Well, I suppose we could, but we'd look fairly ridiculous when we wrote our address in the campsite's register and revealed that we live 200 yards up the road.

Oh sod it, I'm off to put the tent up in the garden.

* Just kidding. I love Devon. Sorry, but I do.

Name

2008

Things are quite exciting in our house at the moment. We're enjoying the patter of tiny feet. And they're not webbed ones, for a change. The geese will have to take a back seat for a bit, because it's real little human feet we've got. Four of them, attached to twin boys.

And since they arrived, the world has been full of surprises. That nice Mr Darling is giving us £250 to start a trust fund. Friends with rapidly growing children are jettisoning unneeded babycare items in our direction like they're going out of fashion. But possibly the biggest surprise of all is our total inability to come up with suitable names for them. A Christian name is important. You have to get it right. It's someone's whole life you're dealing with. Two lives in this case.

On a practical level our surname precludes certain options. William's no good, because his initials would be WC. I love the name Ross, but Ross Cross? Brent's definitely out, as would Victoria be if they were girls. And certainly not Christopher. I've tried to remember any inspirational Crosses I've met over the years, but there really haven't been very many. And we're not fans of the modern trend of naming children after alcopops or deliberately misspelling an otherwise perfectly normal name (the intention being, I presume, to confound the primary school teachers of the future and give the child some sort of self-perceived exclusivity).

Maybe I'm over-analysing things. Surely the implications of a name are pretty meaningless anyway, as long as it sounds nice. In Africa we met countless people with what we initially thought to be amusing names. We met a charming man in his sixties called Socks. We met an Ornament, a Trymore, and his brother Tryharder, a Hatred, a Jealous, a Neveragain. Oh, and a poor chap who sheepishly introduced himself as Adolf. Now although we may find these names funny, the fact is that Ornament is a nice-sounding word. Nothing more. It's a good name. What's the difference between someone whose first language isn't English calling their child *Ornament*, and an English person with little knowledge of angicised 7th century Gaelic calling their child *Kevin*?

Of course the most tempting option is something Cornish. After all, I have actively discouraged the missus from leaving Cornwall for the last few months for fear that the poor children's first view of the world be somewhere other than the crumbling interior of Treliske hospital. Heaven forbid that he/she might one day have to utter those dread words, "No, I *am* Cornish, but my mother happened to be visiting friends in Milton Keynes when I came along, so I wasn't actually born here". I mean, *anyone* could say that, couldn't they? Who's going to check?

On the hunt for good Cornish names, though, it's becoming apparent that girls' names are better. There are loads of lovely ones: Loveday, Kerensa, Lamorna, Lowenna. And let's not forget the queen of Cornish girls' names, Demelza (actually tarnished a little by the fact that Winston Graham made it up for a book in 1945. Racking his brains for the ideal name to give his Poldark heroine as he drove along the little road that was then the A30, he saw the sign for the hamlet of Demelza and had his Eureka moment. As far as I know it only became a common name when the TV show popularised the books in the mid-seventies. I could be wrong, but I've never met a Demelza in her forties).

Cornish boys' names are a different matter. Denzil's great, but somewhat stigmatised by all those Jethro jokes about Denzil Penberthy. There's Jago, the Cornish version of James. And Jowan, the Cornish John. Straightforward Cornish place names can be good, but you need the right one (sample classroom conversation circa 2015: "Ventongimps Cross! Give Chablis her crayon back!" No, I don't think so). Piran's nice, though it seems a little odd to name a Cornish boy after an Irishman. And Samson, although ideally you want to be a strapping great bloke to carry that one off. Perfect if either of them ends up captaining the Pirates. Well, I can dream can't I?

Looking back through my family records it seems that the most popular boys' names were always a bit, well, *normal*. I'm realising that if you want a Cornish-sounding name, you really can't go wrong with Richard. Or James. Or John. That's what chaps in my family have always been called. And when I look through my book of olde worlde Cornish boys' names they're all too hardcore Celtic. Too Lord of the Rings. I mean, Elek?

Dogho? Morvargh? All great names for dragonslayers. Pyrk could certainly lead to problems in the playground.

We seem to be getting nowhere with this. Like a pair of wide-eyed bunnies sitting in the road staring transfixed at the blinding halogen spotlights of the speeding Range Rover that is the spectre of the six-week deadline for registering a name, we seem to be analysing every idea at length, then discarding it for one reason or another. Those boys need names. Friends and relatives are getting twitchy. And time's running out.

We ended up with two names that aren't Cornish at all. Jewish Old Testament in fact. Ah, but we rather overcompensated with their middle names: Seth Trevelyan and Benjamin Trelawny.
Proper job.

Tourist

2005

There's no doubt about it, travel really does broaden the mind. Exploring and learning about your own country as well as other people's makes you a better, more interesting person. Everyone who has the slightest inclination should try to travel as much as possible. You'll die happier.

But there's a downside. It means you have to be a tourist. And no-one wants to be one of those. There's an unspoken, undeniable stigma about the word. Sweeping generalisations are made about all tourists. 'American tourist' means nasty Hawaii shirt and a range of expensive cameras rattling against a severely distended belly, right? German tourists do that thing with their towels on the sun loungers. And of course 'English tourist' conjures up visions of knotted hankies and kiss-me-quick hats, or sweaty young pink people marauding the streets of some doomed Greek resort, crazed on cheap booze and their unfettered libidos.

It doesn't matter how admirable your reasons are for visiting a place, or how much the locals need your money, there will always be a part of you that suspects, deep down, that they despise you, and wish you weren't there. Whenever we opt to become a tourist for a week or two, we always know that it's going to be a tiny bit, well, *embarrassing*.

And it doesn't help that you know you'll spend the first week of your holiday nurturing and then shedding a layer of scarlet skin because you underestimated the sun, again. And then you'll have lots of fun with the wacky currency, trying to remember whether you take off two noughts and divide by three, or divide by three and take off two noughts, so you're not constantly handing barmen 3p for a round of drinks and £20 to taxi drivers for a tip.

Some tourists simply don't give a damn. They just carry on regardless, unashamed of who they are, and oblivious to the fact that the locals are laughing at them sitting in the midday sun, going purple. But most of us do care, and go to some lengths to confront that nagging suspicion that we're being looked down upon.

The most common technique we use is disguise. One simply pretends to be a local. Now, dressing and behaving in such a way as to give the impression you've lived somewhere all your life is all very well, if you get it right. But it can go badly wrong if you're not sure what you're doing, and can leave you looking a bit of a fool. When it's a foreign country, with its unfamiliar culture, you've got to be careful. I've seen the rich Americans on safari in Africa, ironed and pressed, khaki-chic-clad, pristine little penknives hanging in special holsters on belts, desperate to blend in, but standing out like a sore thumb. I did it myself when backpacking around Canada in my twenties. Clad in padded plaid shirt, big boots and baseball cap, I thought I fitted right in. No chance of me being mistaken for an ignorant British tourist, I thought. After several months of strutting about like this, it slowly dawned on me that I in fact resembled nothing more than a rather unconvincing extra in *The Deer Hunter*. Any self-respecting Canadian twentysomething was desperate to get away from this old-fashioned redneck clichéd Canadian image. If I'd have been wearing what I wore back home, I'd have passed for a native Canuk, no sweat.

In Cornwall, tourists have no such trouble, as they're very familiar with the culture. Telling the difference between the tourists and the locals these days has become pretty well impossible, because everyone's gone 'Cornish Casual'. In fact Cornish culture seems to have permeated the nation generally. And so they come pre-tanned, laden with surfboards on roofs, the right sunglasses, the right shoes, and of course those funny beachy trousers that aren't exactly shorts, and come down to below your knees, with lots of little loops, and eyelets with bits of elastic that tighten up for no apparent reason. Trousers that look great when on or close to the beach, but when worn in any other situation reduce the wearer to a self-conscious and rather awkward fashion victim.

It can be a bit disconcerting. A friend of mine on holiday here last summer noticed a couple of 'locals' precariously perched on some rocks near Cadgwith, fishing. Great musclebound specimens they were, shirtless, bronzed, hopping about like mountain goats, apparently comfortable with the tides and enjoying some considerable success. Eventually they packed up and began to make their way home, passing my friend. Bracing himself for a tirade of unintelligible Cornish colloquialisms he asked them what they'd caught. One of them piped up, in a squeaky but enthusiastic Yorkshire accent, "Ah dawnt knaw. A fonny greeny won, and won with t't fin ont top!"

All I'm saying is, be careful who you ask for directions.

Pen

2005

I was sitting here the other day, poking aimlessly at the keyboard, when I became distracted. Creative impasse, writer's block, whatever you want to call it. Often the cause of such distraction is an expectant goose patiently tapping her orange beak on the French doors in the hope of being thrown a bit of apple, or, if she's really lucky, a few lettuce leaves. But on this occasion the geese were nowhere to be seen. I was just plain bored. So as I stared into space I did what most bored people do, and reached for something to fiddle with.

Now I don't have much in the way of executive desktop toys, so I lunged at the nearest pen pot and rummaged among the biros. I enjoy a diverse assortment of these humble gizmos, due to the fact that my wife is a nurse, and drug companies veritably shower anyone harbouring the remotest of leanings towards buying their product with logo-splattered freebies. The missus brings the odd one home in her pocket, and they mount up (often in the bottom of the washing machine). They're amazing some of them. All manner of shapes, colours and sizes. Always shamelessly attempting to subliminally seduce overworked medical staff into choosing their product over an identical one with a different name. Zipostrom, Expilat 200, Binkidix F. Meaningless pychobabble to the uninitiated.

138

Sometimes it's torches, but nine times out of ten it's funky little pens. In the case of the particular little pen I started twiddling with, it was both.

For this pen was the most amazing example of the genre I'd yet seen. This company, Zubiblat (or something), had produced the freebie throwaway pen to end all freebie throwaway pens. Never mind executive desktop toys. You could keep your little shiny balls which bang against each other, and your apparently gravity-defying, fibre-optic reverse waterfall on a tasteful plastic stand. This pen, you see, wasn't just a pen. Press the end once, the little ball point pops out. Nothing unusual about that. Now the clever bit. Press it again, the whole endy bit lights up! Rushing with my pen to the cupboard under the stairs I was delighted to observe a bluey glow illuminating an area of paper around the pen's nib equivalent to, oh, at least a couple of postage stamps. This was too much.

But the novelty value didn't end here. The magic pen had more to give. The bit you held was actually squidgy! It was so malleable that it moulded to the shape of your fingers, providing you with the ultimate in writing comfort. I reckon you could have written for days on end with this thing, without risking the slightest possibility of chafing, blistering or any of the friction-related injuries to which we writers are so tragically susceptible (or were, in the days when we used to use pens). Truly, this was so much more than a mere pen.

Now, being a bloke, I wrote my name with it a couple of times, then took it apart to see how it worked. It never worked again, obviously, because three tiny batteries went flying across the room, and I could only locate two, and there seemed to be a weeny spring missing too, so it didn't go click anymore when I put it back together. Never mind, it was free anyway. What I did learn was that it had a really impressive number of clever little moving parts.

Now it's true a pen like this could probably be found in one of those catalogues that regularly comes to your door, usually hand-delivered by a person who suggests you purchase something as this will directly prevent him from seeking alternative employment doing lots of crimes. But that's not the point. The point is that they can produce these amazing pens somewhere foreign, probably for less than a penny each. It's testament to modern Man's ingenuity. This little pen stands as a simple example of our capabilities as we romp through the second half of the first decade of the still futuristic-sounding 21st century. There's cloning, the internet, massive advances in cancer care, margarine that reduces your cholesterol, and now the illuminating, squidgy Zubiblat free biro. Our genius knows no limits.

Seems a shame, then, that no-one ever invented a sign on Goss Moor saying 'Caution: Low Bridge' which could be read and understood by drivers of tall lorries. And now we'll never know if it was ever possible, because they're bypassing it. This modest yet surprisingly challenging task will remain consigned to the history books forever as the elusive holy grail of inventions. If only someone had asked the people at Zubiblat, they'd have got their people onto it. I can just imagine it: bathed in an ultraviolet glow you'd have to be blind to miss, a subtle sponsor's logo at the bottom, front page headlines reading, 'New sign on A30 spells end to August traffic misery!' And, best of all, relieved truck drivers could pick up a complimentary Zubiblat biro when they stopped at the Little Chef as a reward.

You always think of these things when it's too late.

Coast path

2006

I've been walking the coast path a fair bit this summer. Ah, the coast path. Cornwall's best kept secret, as long as you make sure you get at least 200 yards from any car park or town. Or Lands End. After that you can start to relax. The incidences of dog poo start to dwindle, and you can be confident that you'll only see a handful of like-minded people the whole day. The scenery, needless to say, is world class. Literally breathtaking. But sometimes you get even more than you'd bargained for.

When I walked the Gurnards Head section, for example, I felt as if a David Attenborough series was being enacted all around me. For a start the sea was alive with basking sharks. Great grey battleships of fish, the second-largest in the world, quietly grazing their way through the plankton, vast dorsal fins glinting in the sun, tails flailing, propelling them with stately dignity through the surface chop. Some were alone, some were in twos or threes.

Then, as I was watching two of them quite close in, a beautiful raven flew right past me. And simultaneously a female peregrine landed with a squeal on a gatepost no more than fifty yards away. I didn't know where to look first. Talk about spoilt for choice.

But as I walked the Porthcurno to Penzance leg, it wasn't so much the natural history that blew me away. I was descending into a fishing cove whose identity I shall withhold for reasons which will soon become apparent. I noted the guidebook described it as 'unspoilt'. Now 'unspoilt' is probably the most overused word in all holiday-based literature, so I kept an open mind. But in this case 'unspoilt' was something of an understatement. Like a tiny version of, say, Cadgwith, it was indeed pretty, original, and, well, *unspoilt*. Every building was as I imagined it would have been a hundred or so years ago.

But the experience was to go way beyond the picture postcard thing. It was to become a unique moment in time. I hadn't seen a soul on the walk so far (having started walking at 7am due to the local bus schedule), so having spent the morning exclusively in the company of stonechats and fulmars, any human encounter was destined to be meaningful. On the tiny beach were two fishermen, both of mature years, calmly unloading the morning's haul in bins from their old boat. I was transported back through time. Very little about this scene couldn't have been a hundred years ago (OK, the bins were plastic, and they were loading them onto the back of a small van, but apart from that it had all the features of a classic Cornish scene). Never mind a hundred years, those men looked as if they'd been doing it for a thousand. At 8am on a humid summer morning, with the gulls screaming overhead, and these two salty sea dogs harvesting the fruit of their pots, it could have been a page of Daphne du Maurier, or a Stanhope Forbes painting. Just one perfect moment, frozen in time.

Of course my 21st century mind couldn't help considering practicalities. Where were the lobsters heading? If it hadn't been such a perfect, uninterruptible moment, and if the salty old sea dogs hadn't looked so engrossed in what they were doing, and if I wasn't planning to walk in sweltering temperatures for the next five hours, I'd probably have attempted to chat. Maybe even procure something fishy from them. But in that heat the thing would be steaming by the time I reached Penzance, and besides it wasn't as if you couldn't buy the odd bit of fish there. And, Cornish though I am, I couldn't help feeling like a vulgar intruder peering into their world. I thought of that classic scene in Bill Forsyth's 1983 film, *Local Hero*, when the rich Texas oilman admires the local fishermen's haul of lobsters in the harbour of a remote Scottish village.

"Don't you eat them?" he asks them, enthusiastically. The fishermen look upon him with incredulity and reply, "Oh no. Too expensive!"

So as I passed them I opted for the standard traditional Cornish greeting for this sort of situation:

"All right?"

And its traditional reply:

"All right?"

And that was that. Those two fishermen, I imagine, didn't give the moment a second thought. They were too busy working; probably doing sums in their heads, weighing the catch, thinking about which pots needed mending, and about a thousand other things. I'm sure they were used to being photographed, but I bet the idyllic nature of this scene was not their primary concern. There's nothing idyllic about trying to make a living as a fisherman in Cornwall, after all. And every day is not a flat calm sunny morning in August.

As I walked on, the poignancy of that scene saddened me a little. It was only so enthralling because one no longer expects to witness such a scene these days. But that fifteen minutes had transported me. That tiny, fleeting, romantic snapshot of a world gone by was the highlight of an eleven mile walk. The day a Stanhope Forbes painting had come to life.

Two-stroke

2007

Everyone's talking about the summer of 2007, just as they did about the summer of 2006. But for very different reasons. No-one can deny it's been a disappointing one, although I'd argue that in Cornwall it's been no worse than plenty of other rubbish summers.

So let's cheer ourselves up by thinking about the very essence of summer. As is often the case, it's the smells which bring it all to life. Ah, the smells of summer: if you could bottle them they'd be more useful than any February skiing holiday for getting you through the endless winter months. And now I'm wondering, what is the absolute, quintessential summer smell? What olfactory sensation is so fundamentally, essentially *summery*, that, if you could only experience it on the direst, darkest winter's night, you'd be spontaneously transported straight to a warm July evening?

For me there are several contenders. High on the list would have to be coconut-scented gorse bushes. Hot suntan oil combined with a background whiff of seaweed and salt would have to be up there too. And how about the sickly, slightly on-the-turn aroma of vanilla ice-cream, melted on a hot hand and left there, unlicked, for a little too long? Obviously you'd have to include freshly mown grass on the list. Then there are less obvious ones. The distinctive waft of hot marram grass combined with the merest hint of dog poo on a sandy beach track. I didn't say it had to pleasant, did I? It's a personal thing, obviously. I'm sure we each have our own preference, and it's all based on our own very individual memory.

As far as I'm concerned, there's one summer smell that stands head and shoulders above all the others: the exhaust fumes from a two-stroke engine. Now there is a truly evocative scent, the distinctive discharge from that unique cocktail of petrol and oil. It is so many things combined, and reminds me of countless experiences in my life, all associated with the summer. Two-stroke smoke was the smell of the motor boats on Newquay's Trenance boating lake. What a mighty leap it was as a child to be allowed a go on one of these grown-up machines, when all I'd been previously allowed was a go on the infantile paddle boats. Then there was my dad's old two-stroke Suffolk Punch cylinder lawnmower. Always a devil to start, it was all worth it when you heard that life-affirming pupupup, combined with the sweet perfume emanating from its tiny little red hot exhaust pipe.

Most 16-year-old boys in the seventies spent a lot of time in a fug of two-stroke as this was the heady scent bilging from the back end of the *Fizzie*. That is, the Yamaha FS1-E, 49cc steed of choice for rebellious schoolboys. It was a real bike, the Fizzie. It may have only had 4 horsepower, but to us it enjoyed the kudos of a Triumph Bonneville. Truly an icon of the seventies. Course I never had one as I was nowhere near cool enough. But I spent a lot of time sniffing them. A year or two later and we were into the world of real motorcycles. How well I remember my first ride on the back of a friend's liquid cooled two-stroke 250. Perched on the tiny, brick sized plinth that pretended to be a pillion seat, my knees now inches from my face, suddenly becoming aware that the front wheel had parted company with the road, the bike's tiny engine screaming for mercy as the familiar blue haze flowed from its backside. Ah, happy, summer days, filled with two-stroke.

There followed countless summers messing about on the Carrick Roads in Ern's little flat-bottomed Dory. Clinging to an old bucket handle which we'd tied to a rope towed from the back of the boat, we mastered the technique of standing up on an old surfboard many years before I ever heard the word 'wake boarding'. All the while we were, of course, breathing in lungfuls of the customary smoke from the 40hp outboard.

Looking back, it feels like no summer was complete without that familiar background drone, so cruelly likened to a wasp in a tin can, and its concomitant lingering haze. And now it's 2007, and not much has changed, really, apart from the carbon emissions guilt that now accompanies any mechanised activity. Whether it's the kids racing up our hill on their scooters, or the neighbours trimming the verge with their petrol strimmer, or the distant whine from the *Run What Ya Brung* drag racing event over on Portreath airfield, two-stroke fug is still the smell of the summer to me. And it always will be.

Echium

2009

There was an item in a national newspaper last year about a chap who'd successfully grown a rare and exotic plant in his garden.

He'd apparently brought some seeds back from a family holiday in Madeira, cleverly managed to germinate some in his greenhouse under strictly-controlled conditions, successfully brought several straggly seedlings on, one of which made it to adulthood, and was now displayed proudly in his garden in Neasden. Or Newbury, or somewhere. Upcountry anyway. 'People have occasionally managed to grow them in the UK before,' said an expert in the article. 'But this is a particularly fine example.'

In the accompanying photo there was this proud old chap standing in the middle of his front lawn, his spindly horticultural triumph tottering precariously in a plastic pot next to him, barely any higher than the man himself. The picture put me in mind of old lithographs of the great plant hunters: he could have been Joseph Hooker, returning from some malarial plant-hunting expedition and unloading the first rhododendron, plonking it down on the quayside and exclaiming, "There you go then, I call 'em rhododendrons. Reckon they'll catch on?"

So what was it that the old gent had grown, I hear you cry. Some rare epiphytic bromeliad? Some precious variegated orchid? The first truly blue rose? No. A flipping *echium*, that's what. The *pininana* one, which a friend of mine who is a master of understatement refers to as the 'Cornish foxglove'. Even non-gardeners know them: those colossal, phallic spikes of tiny cobalt flowers which loom out at us from Cornish borders and hedges, lolloping giants' fingers thrusting skywards throughout the early summer. Go down to the big public car park on the seafront in Penzance in June and tell me the *echium* is a hard plant to grow.

It's becoming an increasingly common part of the landscape down here. Which is hardly surprising, as it can transform the humblest miner's cottage garden into an enviable sub-tropical statement. In the pursuit of the sexy exotic planting scheme, *echium pininana* has few rivals. Brighter and less common than the ubiquitous *cordyline* palm, it's less fussy and far happier in poor soil than a tree fern, and faster-growing and bigger than those oh-so-slow, dangerously spiky *agaves*.

It also represents amazing value for money. I've grown dozens, and never spent a penny on any. All you do is dig up a few seedlings from a consenting friend's garden when they're a few inches high, or lie a dead one down in your garden as it goes to seed, wherever you want them to grow. The following year there's your little patch of freshly germinated new *echium*s. Then you just watch them, skulking in the shadows at this time of year like moody teenagers, waiting for their moment to step up and shine. And when the moment is right, they shoot jaw-droppingly for the stars, flowering spectacularly, drawing admiring gazes from all who pass. Then they just lose the will to live, fall over and set seed. As a biennial you know they are doomed from the start, but they are just so wacky, and surreal, and different to everything else that you just have to have one. Sort of like a botanical DeLorean.

The *echium* is now so popular in Cornwall that I'd like to put it forward as a contender for the controversial new Super Council logo. With a chough perched on it of course. I must admit it wouldn't actually be very Cornish, what with the chough still being one of the rarest birds in Cornwall, and *echiums* originating in the Canary Isles. But no-one could deny that a chough/*echium* in front of the 15 bezants would make a lot more sense than that meaningless, generic-looking yellow cartoon flame thing they seem to be going with.

The fact that upcountry the *echium* remains a newsworthy horticultural rarity confirms what we gloating Cornish have always suspected: that things *are* better down here because it's warmer and, well, just plain *nicer*. I used to have to rely on my wife's aunt's annual visit to remind me of this. Every year when she comes to stay from upcountry, I give her a little succulent *aeonium* 'Schwartzkopf' in a pot. And every year, right at the end of her stay, she sheepishly comes and asks for another one because she's killed the previous year's by leaving it outside for too long. But I refrain from shouting at her, because, as I hand her a new plant, I quite enjoy that warm and perfectly harmless Cornish smug feeling.

It's hard to believe that things can really be *that* much warmer in Cornwall than upcountry, but nowhere is it more apparent than when one gazes upon a bed of *echium pininana*. Our friend in Newbury/Neasden is doing a very nice job for our Cornish pride. This isn't just the country's top tourist destination; it's a place where such exotica flourishes effortlessly in hedgerows. Well, it does normally. But then once in a while one of those freakishly cold Siberian winters comes along, like the one we appear to be having now. As I write I'm gazing upon a bed of about twenty echiums, and I have to say they are not looking good. Ah well, I suppose we Cornish have to have our bubble burst every once in a while.

Christmas lunch

2008

A nother year gone, another Christmas looming. The twins are almost a year old. And therein lies a problem.

My wife's vegetarian philosophy is absolutely irrefutable (that killing an animal is seriously bad news if you happen to be the animal), and she doesn't want any part in it. It's as basic as that. You really can't argue with something so straight-forward. People do sometimes attempt to argue with her that the animal wouldn't have existed in the first place if it wasn't for the meat industry. Which is no argument at all, because it just makes the whole thing even more cruel. And sometimes people think it's hilarious to say things like "But what about the carrots? Vegetables have feelings too!" Which is a) not at all funny, and b) a stupid thing to say, on account of vegetables' perfectly obvious lack of a central nervous system. And some people even claim that meat is OK because it's a byproduct of the leather industry, which we all need. To which the obvious reply is, "Not if you don't buy leather you don't".

I reckon she's 100% right. But I am a far weaker and more self-indulgent person, and have killed too many pigeons and rabbits and fish (in my pre-reform days of course), and just like meat too much. So I compromise by generally eating meat which I'm fairly certain has had a good life. Well, good right up to the point at which it is prematurely ended in a moment of blind terror. Anyway, my wife and I rub along quite well, for two people at opposite ends of the humanitarian scale.

As far as the twins are concerned, we've been skirting around the issue of their long-term diet for almost a year now. Up to now they've been fully vegetarian, which is quite easy because they consume mostly gungy gloop (paradoxically referred to as 'solids'). They don't know what they're missing, yet, and wouldn't be able to tell us if they did, so that's OK. But the clock's ticking.

We have toyed with a few options for their dietary future. They could have one day on, one day off (pork chop on Monday...mung bean and nut medley on Tuesday...nice bit of fish Wednesday...veggie burger Thursday...). but that's not really satisfactory. And we've joked that we could bring one up veggie like his mother and one a filthy meat eater like his weak and unprincipled old man. The ultimate controlled experiment: and just the sort of thing they do with identical twins, or so I'm told. Conventional thought dictates that one twin would then grow up a namby-pamby, lentil-munching, pasty-faced wearer of sandals, the other a rosy-chacked prop forward man's man who never feels the cold. But, judging by the vegetarian children I know, that's rubbish.

I do feel that there would be something fundamentally wrong about a Cornish boy not ever knowing what a bit of mackerel tastes like. Or crab, or a meat pasty, or fish and chips.

And now it's Christmas, which as we all know is the season of Bringing Things to a Head. And yet we're both still burying our heads in the sand, because we know that it's a point of principle for both of us. I did do the whole nut roast and vegetarian gravy thing one year and, whilst I'm sure it's perfectly delicious for someone who hasn't known the pleasures of dead flesh ingestion for a while, it left me feeling rather sad and empty. And, to be honest, not very Christmassy. Whilst my wife wouldn't want the boys to contaminate their little alimentary canals with the flesh of something which was once a happy creature, the bleak fact is that for the vast majority of us, a traditional family Christmas simply isn't the same unless a larger-than-necessary bird dies.

Not that it has to be a turkey. A friend of ours always tucks into a tasty lobster for Christmas; an idea I've always rather liked. It's got a nice ring to it, a traditional Christmas lobster, with all the trimmings. Unfortunately goose is out of the question since a gaggle of them became part of the family eight years ago. I'd have to question the mental security of a person who could spend £150 getting the vet to put a pin into their pet goose's broken leg, and then happily shove fistfuls of Paxo up their rear end come December. I'm afraid these days I fall into the first camp.

Ah well. Whatever the twins end up having, it'll probably just get chucked into the blender and turned into gloop anyway, so it doesn't make much odds. Maybe we can avoid the subject for another year. Happy Christmas.

Baffled

2006

T here have been a number of things baffling me of late. I'm not sure why. In fact I'm even baffled as to why I'm so baffled. Maybe as you get older you don't get wiser; you just understand the world less. I'm not talking about the big things. I'm talking about the tiny things. And if I can't grasp why so many people think that shower gel is preferable to a bar of soap, then I'm quite a way off ever getting a grip on international politics.

I'm baffled by pasta. It comes in every conceivable shape, to be used in different dishes, yet they all taste exactly the same. You must use *spaghetti* for *spaghetti alla carbonara* and *fettucine* for *fettucine all' alfredo,* and heaven forbid you should ever try mixing the two and attempting *spaghetti all' alfredo.* No-one's ever been able to explain to me why that is, other than the spurious claim that the sauce sticks to the different surfaces slightly differently.

And I'm baffled as to why, as soon as a politician makes a mistake, the media comes down on them like a ton of bricks, trying to humiliate them from every angle, removing any trace of respect we might once have had for them. And then the same media then condemn our youth for not being bothered to vote in elections because they don't respect politicians.

I'm baffled at the fact that a human being could ever have said, "Let's make sick people arriving for an appointment pay to park their car outside the hospital".

I'm baffled that, in a country so developed that practically all our roads are tarred, and where fuel prices are tottering towards £4 a gallon, so many people choose to drive a huge great expensive all-terrain truck with twice the fuel consumption of a normal car. Maybe they're trying to create the illusion of a person whose property is so vast and untamed that a four wheel drive is a necessity just to get to and from it. It's baffling, especially when I recall that year we spent driving on dirt roads in Africa. After more than thirty thousand miles and eight countries, the missus and me had experienced one slow puncture, and got briefly stuck in sand on two occasions. What mighty road tool had we selected for such a task? A Nissan Sunny (yep, we'd reckoned that we'd have no trouble sourcing spare parts for one of the commonest cars in southern Africa, plus those parts would be cheap). That car didn't let us down once. So if a nice sensible family saloon was perfectly adequate for such an adventure, why do so many British drivers find it necessary to clog our roads with these silly, over-engineered leviathons?

Back to soap v shower gel. It feels as if I'm the only one who appreciates that the humble bar of soap is the most perfect of inventions. I can't imagine a better example of efficient ergonomics. So why, when we're in the shower, have we given up using that trusty bar of soap, in favour of wrestling with the stopper of an ungainly plastic bottle of shampooey gunk which washes away almost immediately? Perhaps the person who can adequately explain it can also explain the success of the weird-shaped, funny-angled, bendy toothbrush with ten different types of bristles and a thing on the back that scrapes stuff off your tongue. Honestly, if it was that good an idea don't you think someone would have thought of it before now? As innovations go, it's not that impressive.

Finally, I'm baffled as to why South West Water is digging up the road outside my house again even though they've already done it twice this year. Perhaps they're going for some kind of record. I did try ringing the helpline, explaining, "There's a hundred yards of bollards, barriers and great big holes. I've had traffic lights outside my gate for over a month and everyone in my road is affected".

"No, I have no record of when the job might end," said the helpful girl on the helpline, helpfully.

"Can you tell me anything about the job at all?" I asked.

"Um, no," she replied, "There's no record of any work in that area. Is there anything else I can help you with today?" What did she mean, "*Else*"?

Maybe it's good to be baffled. It makes life more interesting, and instills in all of us a sense of wonder. Or maybe users of shower gel simply know something I don't. Maybe the ghastly upheaval on my road will turn out to represent some kind of perverse value for money. Perhaps South West Water's making an extra effort to make our water really special. Perhaps it'll come out fizzy, or with a hint of elderflower.

You'd think so, for seven hundred quid a year.

Townies

2009

Recently I was reading an article written by a man who'd moved with his wife and three kids to rural New Zealand in pursuit of the good life, only to leave and move back to the city after a year because, it seems, he just got bored. "After a year in the pristine seclusion of Golden Bay tending the veg plot," he said, "I crave the infernal stink of the big city, and the juice inducing competition of the rat race".

Now this chap had previously been the *Telegraph*'s South Asia correspondent, so one assumes he wasn't stupid. And his experience of living in New Zealand appeared to have lived up to his expectations in every way. He simply didn't like it. And was never going to like it, because he was quite plainly never cut out to live somewhere so rural.

He needed to be in a city.

'*Townie*' is a word we Cornish have used a lot over the years. It's usually used disparagingly, even condescendingly, to describe a person who is more at home in a concrete jungle than one with, well, trees. It's a particularly relevant word for us to use down here though, because we have no big towns, and therefore you couldn't, by definition, have a Cornish *townie*. It would be an oxymoron. Neighbouring Devon, rural and lovely as it is, has a couple of proper cities. You can be a townie in Devon. In Cornwall, even when you're in one of our bigger towns, it still feels like the country.

Isn't this one of the great things about living here? It's a major factor contributing to our feeling of uniqueness. Unlike our friend in New Zealand, we generally know what we want in Cornwall. We want to feel close to the outdoors, even when we're not in it. And we want other things; a mild climate, people to say hello in the street, and to know that the sea is never far away. We like the feeling that we are different. It may be an intangible feeling, but we feel it. We are separate from the rest of the country, both geographically and spiritually. We like that. We like the fact that Cornwall is no place for townies.

Truro, of course, could ultimately become the fly in our idyllic rural ointment. Already oddly labelled a city, on account of the Victorian cathedral, it's looking like a prime contender to become a serious, upcountry-sized town. It would have to grow tenfold to rival Plymouth, but the proposed *Truro and Threemilestone Area Action Plan* development could add a whopping 6,000-odd houses to the little town in which generations of my family grew up.

I sometimes wonder about city-minded types who, for whatever reason, find themselves residing in Cornwall. Can it ever really be what they want? I suppose you do see adverts for yuppie flats, sorry, *apartments*, overlooking the silted-up Truro mudfats, promoting this as some sort of sophisticated urban lifestyle choice. But isn't this rather missing the point? I mean, most of us just aren't really into that sort of thing down here. That's why we love it. For most of my years in London I was working in **Covent Garden**, and I can tell you, for this Truronian, that **urban culture** had a limited appeal.

But maybe a **desire for an** urban lifestyle is just symptomatic of today's **way of life. These** days we all want to have our cake, eat it, and **have a spare in** the cake tin, with cherries on. We want everything, all at the same time. Today's sophisticated **metrosexual in** Cornwall wants to sit in a neon-lit bar sipping his **mochaccino-latte**, checking his expensive hairdo in the reflection **of his** iPhone one minute, belting to the north coast to go **kitesurfing the** next, back in time for happy hour. Let's call it **progress**.

Actually, that **doesn't sound** so bad. Maybe I'm just jealous.

Display logs

2011

I've noticed a curious phenomenon over the past year. I first became aware of it whilst watching the Chelsea Flower Show TV coverage last spring. Usually it's nice to find out what's going to be the next big thing, garden wise. But last year I spotted something a bit surprising lurking in the background of all the Chelsea show gardens.

Log piles. No, not that kind of log pile. Not a mere pile of logs. Something much more refined. I'm talking about immaculately stacked, identical little logs, meticulously arranged within a specially constructed storage area, their ends so perfectly even that you'd swear someone had taken an orbital sander to them. A bona-fide garden feature in itself.

And now I keep seeing these things in living rooms too. Yes, rather than the more traditional practice of dumping a basket of mucky, old, randomly split logs by the woodburner and cringing as an entire entomological ecosystem runs for the cover of the sofa, the strange, immaculate log-stack concept has moved indoors. Wherever you see an appropriate alcove, there they are, demanding our attention, saying, 'I may essentially be just a pile of logs, but I've been carefully selected, and now you're looking at me in a whole new light, aren't you? And I'm actually rather beautiful, aren't I?'

Let's be honest, the logs most of us burn don't tend to look like this. Whilst I'll admit there's something very pleasing about a neatly stacked pile of logs, they are, by definition, utilitarian. It is fuel for the winter. Nothing more. The logs sit outside, or in a shed, and then you bring some in and burn them to warm yourself/cook on. Even if you are organized enough to neatly stack your logs up against a wall or something, they're still always going to be hanging with bits of bark and woodlice, and moss, and nondescript blackish organic material. The average basketful of logs in my house contains everything from 4x2 building job remnants splattered with old nails, to prunings from last year's buddleia cull, to bits I've found whilst out on walks and chucked in the boot of the car. So my winter fuel is consistent in neither shape nor quality. You wouldn't want to try stacking it at all, never mind ask someone to admire it.

I'm not sure what it all means. What are we trying to say to the world by displaying our winter fuel in such a way? Who in their right mind would take such care to store their logs in such a fastidious fashion, if all they are going to do is set light to them?

Ah, but there's the rub. I don't think these lucky logs are ever even going to be troubled by a box of matches. And I have proof, because a friend of ours has such a feature in her front room. The other day she was shocked to discover her house guests had come home before her and used them to start a fire: "They used my display logs!" she exclaimed. Yes, you read it right. Display logs. So now we have a name for this lunacy.

Which brings us to further questions. Where do devotees of these 'display logs' actually store their real logs? You know, the ones they're actually planning to, er, *set light to*. And another obvious question: Display logs must be an awful dust trap, mustn't they (unless you display them behind glass of course, which presumably isn't out of the question)? So do you have to hoover your logs, and pray nobody walks in on you?

I don't know. We all have things we will never understand the point of. Avocadoes. Sport utility vehicles. The Cornish Pasty Association. Kerry Katona. Belgium. Those I can live with. But I truly fear for a world in which there are display logs.

Nobody loves a kleptoparasite

2003

S o the Cornish chough is back where it belongs. In Cornwall. All six of them. There's no-one happier about it than me. The council coat of arms, with its unfortunate gathering of near moribund characters, miner, fisherman and chough, doesn't look so dated anymore, now that the bird that sits atop it is no longer mythological. We got our dodo back. But I've been thinking about it a lot lately; isn't it a little crazy that such a rare, no, *practically nonexistent* creature still has pride of place? It is hundreds of years since the chough was a common sight down here. Surely a more appropriate candidate for the hallowed position could be found. And I think I know just the chap.

Yep, the herring gull. A far more appropriate choice for our official Cornish bird. Gulls are absolutely beautiful, and they do such an underrated job of cleaning up after our own filthy species that they've more than earned their place. Why are we obsessed by the notion that if something is common, it's not as beautiful as a rare thing? When did you last actually look at, say, a magpie? Or meadow cranesbill? If the former was a rare migrant, people would be coming for miles to get a glimpse of the stunning bird. If the latter was a sub-tropical hybrid that's difficult to cultivate people would queue to buy it at the nursery and the RHS would probably give it an Award of Garden Merit.

We should all take another look at gulls. I love them, particularly after living away from this gull mecca for some time. I defy any red-blooded Cornishperson not to get a saffron-scented wave of nostalgia on hearing the cry of a distant gull when away from home. It is, truly, the most evocative sound in the world.

Of course they're not always the best-behaved of creatures, but what do we expect? They can't help it if their feeding habits are technically described as *kleptoparasitic*. I suppose one could argue that being a kleptoparasite isn't the most respectable way to make a living. But hey, we've all got to get by. Ignorant tourists' sustained practice of feeding them is obviously going to lead to certain town gulls hanging around near people. They're not stupid. Far from it. They soon learn that people mean food. So when we see a gull standing on a rubbish bin pulling out old pasty wrappers and chip papers and sprinkling them all over the street, don't be too hard on him. He's really only doing what we've taught him to do. Ninety-nine percent of the time they are happily cleaning up after us. You've really got to put yourself in their shoes.

The only time gulls really worry me is when they mug you in gangs. The psycho gull gang that brutally robbed me of my cod and chips in Mevagissey once was a serious matter. I think they must have been from out of town. Maybe even come down from upcountry to cause some trouble. On motorbikes probably. My friend and I left the chip shop, and as I ravenously unwrapped the sweet-smelling package, I felt a blow to my back. I looked round to get a faceful of flailing wing and, letting my guard down for a split second, another gull brushed the meal out of my hands and onto the ground. I swear they knew exactly what they were doing with that diversionary tactic, and that as soon as food hit ground I would no longer be interested in it. Within seconds a whole flock was upon the abandoned supper. They had it all worked out. I reckon Alfred Hitchcock was right – if birds ever work out what they could achieve with a few organisational skills, look out.

I remember seeing that David Attenborough film of the crows in Tokyo who have trouble opening the hard walnuts growing by a busy road. They press the button on the pedestrian crossing to stop the traffic, place the hard nut under a stationary car tyre, wait for the car to roll over it, press the button again and then pop out and eat the nut, hopping out of the way just before the light turns green again. It makes you think. I know people who wouldn't have thought of that.

Once when I was coming back from Scilly on the Scillonian late in the day, I wondered why there was a flurry of gull activity. Looking down below, I saw that a cook was throwing all the old pasties and sausage rolls out of the kitchen window. Obviously I tried to reach down and catch the odd scrap myself, but having failed, resigned myself to watching the gulls, who were having a good feed. I noticed that several jumbo-sized sausages got lodged on the kitchen windowsill. Several gulls tried to land in that awkward place to grab a sausage, without success due to the speed of the boat.

Twenty minutes later as we approached Penzance harbour the boat slowed down and I watched a young, still-brown gull manage to land on the ledge. Quick and efficient, it picked up a jumbo sausage in its beak crosswise, then in one deft movement flipped it so that it was held, cigar-like, in the end of its beak. And then, marvel of marvels, in one gulp, it swallowed the whole thing. It then did the same thing to three more sausages. I couldn't believe it. It was grotesque. It was disgusting. It was impressive. Four jumbo sausages consumed in under ten seconds. If that had been a person, pound for pound, the weight would have been equivalent to both your legs. After standing there for a second or two and, I imagine, either thinking to himself 'What a feed. I couldn't manage another thing,' or, 'Good Lord, I'm feeling a bit seasick. I never should have had that last sausage,' the heroic bird attempted to take off. I swear it cleared the sea by less than a foot. But made it, just, having practically doubled its own bodyweight.

A bird that can do that gets my vote. If any bird deserves to be our Cornish mascot, standing proud atop our coat of arms, ladies and gentleman I give you the Herring Gull. *Larus argentatus*. It's a survivor, it's integral to the Cornish way of life, and it works for its living. Forget the delicate chough.

Vote gull.

168

Rayburn

2010

After nine years of blindly throwing wads of cash at my local domestic heating oil supplier, I'm very happy to declare that our prehistoric Rayburn has been consigned to the scrapheap.

Well, a corner of the garage, to be exact. I was so angry with the thing in the end that all I wanted to do was drag it out back and take a sledgehammer to it. Experts advised me that, despite the fact that a few years ago I could have sold it for hundreds of pounds, these days you'd be lucky to sell it for scrap. Such is the unpopularity of household appliances with an old fashioned appetite for fossil based fuels, apparently. "It'll just have to be a garden feature then," I said, imagining it in a sunny corner with nasturtiums cascading from its open doors. I liked the thought of it in its benign dotage, nurturing a bit of nature rather than contributing to its demise.

"Over my dead body," replied the missus, correctly pointing out that whenever I attempt to create something a bit bohemian and arty in the garden, it just ends up looking like the Grundys' back yard in *The Archers*. Or at least what we assume the Grundys' back yard in *The Archers* would look like. There are, after all, gardens which look like that all over Cornwall. We've all seen them.

And yet I liked having a Rayburn. Loved it, even. Loved the fact that it was the socially acceptable, more Cornish, nonponcy alternative to its upper class big sister the Aga. Our Rayburn was, in theory, a practical, versatile little powerhouse of a thing. It was an oven, but also kept the ambient temperature of our damp cottage at a bearable level all year, and even had a go at heating a few radiators. As far as I'm aware, no Aga could do such a thing. It was basic and utilitarian, a practical, modern alternative to the even more traditional and prehistoric Cornish Range.

Except that it didn't work. It didn't heat the radiators beyond body temperature, and the first time I tried to fry an egg on it, I gave up after an hour when I looked in the pan and saw a beak and feet forming. If you turned it up high enough to cook on, the water in the cylinder boiled, waking you at night with what sounded like someone exploring the loft cavity and randomly hitting the pipes with a hammer.

We lived with all that for years. But then when I worked out that this unique experience was costing us £5 a day in oil I knew we had to do something.

Don't get me wrong; I'm sure a modern Rayburn is a different animal altogether. But we Cornish don't have modern Rayburns, do we? We have old, knackered ones that were built to run on wood and coal, and then were cheaply converted to burn nice, inexpensive, clean oil in the seventies. And it hasn't really worked, has it? How well I remember the look of knowing incredulity on my grandmother's face when she first saw us doting on our lovely cottagey Rayburn. She knew all about them from her days at the garden cottage on the Penair Estate, near Truro. Who in their right mind would choose to drive a clapped-out Morris Minor when they could have a shiny new, er, Smart Car? Deluded nostalgia, and some sort of skewed idea of a rural idyll, nothing more. Unfortunately Nan didn't live long enough to see us get rid of the thing, but I suspect she's somewhere now fighting the urge to mutter the words, "I told you so".

So there it sits under a tarp in the garage, an outmoded relic of a bygone age, replaced by a state of the art woodburner/ backboiler combo, and two sleek solar panels on the roof. Yet something stops me disposing of it. Maybe they'll come back into vogue. Maybe it'll be worth something one day.

You don't know anyone looking for one, do you? They really are very good.

Veg box

2011

I'm something of a veg box veteran. Admittedly it was probably my vegetarian, eco-aware wife who originally talked me into it, but for ten years now we've been getting a plastic box full of organic who-knows-what delivered to our doorstep on a weekly basis. It's become part of our life.

I think people get veg boxes delivered because it's the closest thing most of us get to living life the way our parents did, ie. consuming things that have not been sprayed, and are, by and large, grown nearby, and therefore *in season*. I mean, we're never going to grow the stuff ourselves these days, are we? Not with the average new house being allocated a garden smaller than a child's sandpit, and a five-year waiting list for anyone contemplating the considerable responsibility of an allotment. Not to mention all that fiddling about with seeds, and compost, and things. And then all that waiting around.

It's probably true to say that you could buy your veg box items cheaper in Tescos, but that's really not the point. You get a veg box delivered for reasons other than economy. Like the solar panels on my roof, I know that it may be years before they pay for themselves. But they just make me feel, well, good about myself. There are a lot worse things you can do with your money.

172

There are, however, a couple of things about veg boxes that drive me to distraction. It's the stuff you get in them that's the problem. In the summer months it's all about overlap. I usually enjoy some modest success at growing salad crops myself, and there's nothing quite as annoying as giving bags of tomatoes away to anyone who comes to the house, just so that you can consume some identical ones you've paid good money for because they've stuffed a bagful in your veg box.

Same thing with rocket, lettuce, broad beans and numerous herb varieties. And apples in the autumn. I know what you're thinking: why don't you let the farm know what you don't want delivered? Well, if I did that, I'd be ringing them weekly with my exacting requirements for that week. They'd soon mark us down as troublemakers and cross us off their list.

Then the arrival of winter heralds the start of endless months battling with an onslaught of rather dreary vegetables. They're all perfectly nice in moderation. It's their relentlessness that gets to me. Weekly deliveries of kale and cauliflower I can handle. But when they're combined with a cabbage and a bag of sprouts, you start to wonder how you're going to cram it all into seven days, and whether there is a member of the brassica family that isn't grown in vast quantities on Cornish organic farms in winter.

And every week, snuggling next to the brassica collection, is a turnip bigger than an adult head. You'd have to consume turnip every day, all winter, to get through it. Eeugh.

I find myself gingerly approaching the familiar green plastic box on a Wednesday morning with the trepidation of a mother approaching the edge of her child's school swimming pool having spotted something small and brown floating in the water. A typical conversation between myself and my wife will then ensue:

Me (poking dejectedly at the box contents): "We got cabbage again. And a huge turnip. And kale. And beetroot."

Wife: "Ah well. Paul next door loves beetroot. And your mum can have the cabbage, 'cause we've still got last week's. And the geese can have another turnip. You know, as a treat."

Me: "But it's not a treat. The geese get the turnip every week. They're fed up with bloody turnips. They need a break."

I'm not that convinced that Paul next door even likes beetroot. I think he just said he quite liked it, about four years ago, and he's too polite to go back now, when we thrust his weekly dose upon him. Good grief, we're all at it. Pretending we can cope. Even the geese.

But at least all these vegetables are, technically, edible. Which is more than I can say for the Jerusalem artichoke. Ah, now that's a subject that requires a whole column to itself.

Safe

2006

There was a very interesting piece in the paper the other day. They'd conducted an experiment in which they took four owners of modern cars, and made them drive an old car. The paper wanted to find out the extent to which today's car drivers have come to rely on the huge range of so called 'active' safety features which apparently come as standard on a modern car. They exhaustively listed the more common examples. A veritable deluge of acronyms it was. There was *SIPS* (side impact protection system), *ESP* (electronic stability programme), *WHIPS* (Whiplash Protection System) and *ABS* (antilock brakes). Then there was *LSD* (limited slip differential) and *DSTC* (dynamic stability and traction control system). I can sense I'm losing you, but stick with me, because it gets interesting.

The ancient car used for the test was a 15-year-old BMW 3 series, which was apparently 'devoid of every modern safety feature'. During the test in the older car, the four guinea pig drivers were forced to deal with various tricky steering and braking situations.

The result? You've guessed it, the drivers were so used to their own cars doing half the work for them that they 'swung about wildly', lost control, and declared the car impossible to keep in a straight line. It wasn't a Model T Ford they were driving. Nor was it a Chieftain tank. And yet they declared this 1990 car, a car that just a few years ago would have been considered perfectly desirable, to be 'like driving a bus'. It seemed to worry them not a jot that they'd allowed themselves to become entirely reliant on their own clever cars' computerised gizmos to keep them from flying off the road every time they incompetently blundered round a bend. They didn't seem embarrassed at all about their failings.

The conclusion appeared to be that with all these 'active' safety features (which the average person is barely aware of), the modern driver can drive as fast and as badly as he or she likes, and get away with it. How comforting. As long as they've got a modern car that is. Heaven help you if you're the one coming the other way round the bend of a narrow lane. OK, the speeding oncoming vehicle probably won't kill you, because of its amazing traction control. But the heart attack it induces probably will.

So with all this labour-saving technical wizardry, let alone all the cruise control, automatic windscreen wipers and 'adaptive forward lighting', how long will it be before we're sanctioning a carefully timed driver's snooze whilst the car drives itself down the fast lane of the M4? That's right, autopilot is surely the only inevitable conclusion to all this advancement. They could call it *TCCI*: Total Control for Comatose Incompetents. At the end of your snooze the car will gently ease you back into consciousness with some whale music and a fresh cappuccino.

And then I started wondering how different it would have been if the newspaper had conducted the test not in the affluent south east, but in the beleaguered south west. Swap those pampered softies at that transport research centre in Berkshire for some Cornish people at Trepiddle airfield and I reckon they'd have responded to the 15-year-old car very differently. I can see it now...

"What a pleasure to have adjustable seats and a heater," said Ivan Trevaskis. "I felt I could drive a hundred miles in it. And a valid MoT was a bonus."

"Marvellous," declared the second driver, a middle-aged woman, upon finishing the slalom. "Took me a while to stop double declutching, but I must admit this 'ere new-fangled synchromesh is some smooth."

The third driver, a dishevelled old man with bale twine for a belt negotiated the skid pan like a pro whilst rolling a cigarette with his left hand. The examiners complimented him on his control. "Well, it helps not havin' to keep your left foot on the brake pedal every time you go past people. The back lights have never worked on my old pickup you see, so you never know when the rozzers might be watchin'."

The wide-eyed fourth driver, a young woman, proclaimed, "When you lock the doors, they all lock at the same time. I've never seen such a thing before. It's fantastic. How much is a super car like this likely to cost you?"

OK, maybe I'm generalising. Not everyone in Cornwall has an old car. These days there isn't nearly such a proliferation of bangers on Cornish roads. Even out of season you still see posh new cars, so that means locals must own them now. But the essential question we have to ask ourselves is, who would we rather have coming round the bend at us on a dark, rainy night: a skilful, alert driver in an old car with no modern active safety features, or a witless, half-asleep driver confidently relying on all the technology 2006 can offer?

Gosh, you'd need *ESP* to answer a question like that.

In the midst
of gorillas

2010

T hey recently remade the commendable eighties radio
series/book, '*Last Chance to See*' as a BBC TV series, in
which Stephen Fry took the place of the late Douglas Adams.
The premise was that Fry and conservationist Mark
Carwardine try to find a list of critically endangered animals in
various parts of the world while they still could.

It was when Fry referred to seeing the mountain gorillas of
Uganda's Bwindi Impenetrable Forest as 'reputed to be the
greatest wildlife encounter on the planet' that it got me
thinking.

I was there, twelve years ago, and I did exactly the same
thing (well, I suspect our experiences differed slightly in that I
didn't have a BBC budget for a charter plane so my journey to
the forest had involved an assortment of chicken buses and
lifts, and instead of a brief, pleasant stay in the BBC's luxury
tented safari camp, I had a sweltering, week-long wait in a
little dome tent with all the other desperate backpackers as our
names climbed slowly up the standby list). It was, just as Fry
suggested, a truly incredible experience. We saw 18 gorillas
from a family group, including a tiny one-year-old who spent

the whole time clambering on and off his mum's back and squealed hilariously as she quietly climbed the nearest tree to fetch him another fig. And we were just yards away from the colossal, potentially terrifying, yet calm and gentle, male silverback. To wait that long, and walk that far, to finally find yourself staring into the eyes of those astounding wild creatures was an occasion when the overused cliché '*life changing*' is completely appropriate.

But I keep thinking about Fry's words, 'Greatest wildlife encounter on the planet'. I don't think I could ever rank the experience at the top of a list of superlative wildlife encounters. I don't really see the point. I mean, I've often seen two seals bobbing in the surf on my local beach. But I've also seen over a hundred seals down at Godrevy. And I've also seen a quarter of a million seals on a single beach in Namibia. So which of those experiences is the best? Superficially, of course, the last one, because there were more seals, and the location was more exotic. But an unexpected encounter with one seal in the sea is every bit as wonderful.

How much you enjoy these wildlife encounters is controlled only by your circumstances at the time. It's entirely existential. Are the ten grizzly bears I saw in one day in Alaska more moving than the badgers I see in my Cornish garden? Not necessarily, because the badgers are in my garden! I've snorkelled in Zanzibar, and I've snorkelled in the rockpools of Newquay. They both have their plusses.

My twin boys remind me of this every day. At two years old, they gaze upon creatures on a daily basis with just as much awe and wonder in their eyes as I had on encountering those Ugandan gorillas. Only yesterday I spent several minutes with them studying a woodlouse climbing up the outside of my house. They were utterly captivated.

I've actually got the perfect personal example to prove my theory. It happened in 2001 in the Cornish mizzle down on the Lizard. It was there that I saw, for the first time, three wild Cornish choughs. I'd waited 39 years for this, and I'd become a bit obsessed, having grown up watching them in the aviary at Newquay Zoo around the time the last one disappeared from the wild in Cornwall. These three wild birds had recently returned to reclaim their historic homeland, and naturally I'd been desperate for a glimpse. I'd seen plenty of choughs, both kinds, all over Europe, but this was so, so different. To me it meant absolutely everything to see one in Cornwall, particularly as I'd only just recently returned back here myself. It was, truly, a perfect moment.

As far as wildlife encounters go, those three Cornish birds were easily up there with those 18 Ugandan gorillas.

Life-affirming

2007

G osh, this is getting out of hand. For several months running I've been upbeat and positive about things. Should I be worried? What of my hard-earned reputation as the disgruntled malcontent, the miserable Cornishman forever whining in the corner about how things used to be better? Well, I don't care. I'm not going to stop now, because I've had another life-affirming experience. And it happened, like most life-affirming experiences, when I was least expecting it.

A couple of months ago I owed a friend a favour. She needed volunteers to spend the day cajoling people into signing a petition. Fine, I thought. It was a very good cause, and one that I heartily believe in. But there was a catch. She'd got permission to nab people as they arrived at the *Ripcurl Boardmasters Unleashed* pop event, in… *Newquay*. Oh no. I was to be plunged right into the sweaty, teeming, gridlocked, vile heart of darkness that is the reality of 21st century Jamiegate Bay. Furthermore I had to attempt to get there (by car, as I'd sold my queue-busting motorcycle that very week), on changeover day in the middle of the school summer holidays. If I made it, I was then to do battle with the suntan cream and testosterone-oozing legions of Bacardi Breezer-fuelled, lurching teenagers, all doubtless screaming for us to get out of the way so that they could get inside and resume their hedonistic journey to self destruction. This, truly, was to be Hell on Earth. I was dreading it.

The day arrived. My heart full of trepidation, I allowed an hour and a half for the fifteen mile journey. I got there over an hour early. The traffic had been fine (using, obviously, as many back roads as I could, and avoiding the town itself). From the initial security guard's cheery greeting, everything from then on was a revelation. After a quick briefing, I began collecting signatures. And it turned out that the Blair/Brown generation of *'don't give a damn about the world leave it to someone else to vote I just can't be bothered rather play computer games and get drunk and vandalise my local amenities'* lost generation of 'yoof' actually *did* give a damn. What's more, they were polite, most of them. They'd say things like, "Of course, mate, anything for a good cause," and "Gotta look after the environment, man". There was the odd exception, obviously. Some were a bit lairy, and a few were too inebriated, or posh, to even look at you, but good grief, they're entitled to a bit of youthful exuberance.

By late afternoon we'd taken a ridiculous number of signatures and I was feeling something akin to elation. I heard myself saying the words, "Think I'll go in and check out a couple of the bands". And then there were further revelations. The event appeared well-organised, genial, and relaxed. There were enough toilets. And they were clean. The food was edible. It was all Mexican wraps, and Australian pies, and smoothies. The vast Atlantic Ocean backdrop gave it a unique, sort of otherworldly atmosphere. Above all, it was just plain friendly.

And what of the music? Well, I must admit that I already knew that one of the performers was Scott Matthews, whom I rather like. He's an unassuming brummie, more geography student than rock god, standing there in a checked shirt and jeans, but making a sound somewhere between John Martyn and Jeff Buckley which, in my book, is a very nice sound indeed. This music was all about authenticity, not fashion. I'd never have thought it possible, but the kids were loving it. This was music that, twenty five years ago I'd have predicted would be dead in the water by now.

Next up were a band who named themselves Guillemots which, me being a bird lover, gave them a head start. Turns out they're heavily influenced by birdsong and have used recordings on their debut album. And if they sound like a bunch of namby pamby wussy birdy nerdy students, they aren't. These birders rocked, and the crowd loved 'em.

I looked around me. I tried to compare it with the crowd at the last event like this I'd been to. And I concluded that the only significant difference is that these days the audience spends an awful lot of time recording the moment. All around me the young people were thrusting mobile phones or digital cameras in the air to get a shot of the musicians. When they'd finished with that, they'd be phoning somebody up, presumably letting their absent friends in on the action, allowing them to share the moment (or rub their noises in the fact that they weren't there). It was all quite sweet really.

I left while I was still on a high, before anything could happen to burst my bubble, not that I felt it would. I drove home with a big smile on my face. The world wasn't such a bad place. There was hope. People were good, not bad. Things hadn't changed that much. This was, truly, life-affirming.

But enough of that. Next month I'll try to be annoyed about something, I promise. I wouldn't want to lose you.

Milly

2005

I n 1980, a terminally ill Steve McQueen made his last film, *The Hunter*. He played a grizzled bounty hunter, close to retirement. As a hobby he kept a collection of old toys, and in one memorable scene as he fiddled with an old model aeroplane, his girlfriend accused him of only liking old things. Narrowing his eyes as only Steve McQueen could, he enigmatically replies, "New things are no good".

I love that line. I wrote some time back about my theory that there are two types of people in this world: those who like new things and those who like old things. I like old things. Well, I did. Now I'm not so sure.

My wife owns a classic car. It's a blue 1956 Morris Traveller called Milly. A Traveller is the one with the wood on the back, for those of you born after 1970 (that's the year they made the last one, after producing over a million of them). It was quite exciting when we first got Milly. One of the vehicles I'd learned to drive in was an ex GPO Morris Minor van, so I was no stranger to the endearing quirks of early 20th century car design. I looked forward to the fun that classic car ownership would no doubt bring. Ludicrous 'foot dip' button? No problem, I'd have hours of amusement baffling wide-eyed passengers as to how I was able to dip the headlights without apparently

186

touching anything. Non-existent heating system? A hat and gloves would see to that. The missus had always loved Morris Travellers, with their adorable ash frame, and their sweet little back doors, and their oodles of character you couldn't possibly get in a modern car. We've had Milly four years now.

Things have been pretty interesting. Every 3,000 miles we jack her up and grease various nipples. We source dealers all over the country for parts (her fourth fuel pump will be fitted this week). Last year the AA started charging us as we'd reached our callout limit. Broken half shaft here, faulty condenser there. We stand in specialist paint shops and thumb through dog-eared old books trying to identify an accurate paint match for touching up. When we couldn't fix a leak in one of her cylinders, the cheapest solution turned out to be bunging another engine in. Come to think of it, the wood is pretty much the only bit that we haven't replaced in four years. We debate the advantages of steel versus fibreglass wings. My latest attempt at maintenance involved Milly's leaky quarterlights. A Morris Minor quarterlight is a design of such improbable complexity that it would have Heath Robinson scratching his head and thumbing through the yellow pages. When I'd finished the job the new rubber quarterlight seals were leakier than when I'd started.

Worst of all, there's the wood. Why oh why did she have to set her heart on a Traveller, the model that, since it was introduced in 1956, has never quite made up its mind if it's a car or a sideboard? If it was the standard saloon version it wouldn't be quite so bad. We constantly sand and oil that

187

infernal crate in a doomed attempt to slow the undeniable fact that Cornish drizzle and forty-something separate pieces of 50-year-old wood do not sit comfortably together. Damn it, there's something very wrong about consulting a cabinet maker when you're trying to fix your car. And it's not as if the wood's merely cosmetic. Take the wood off and the car falls apart. You can fail your MoT if the wood's not up to scratch. I ask you.

And all the time we feel guilty that we don't seem to share the undying dedication to their vehicles that other members of the Morris Minor Owners Club seem to feel. It's like some sort of religion. A faith. As the years go by, you see the thing slowly crumbling, and you know that all you're doing is postponing the inevitable, and that the whole experience is simply a bleak, soul-destroying exercise in crisis management. Soon the desirable Cornish number plate will be the most valuable thing on the vehicle.

I'd never have dared tell him to his face, but Steve McQueen was wrong. New things *are* good. Maybe someone will eventually design a modern version of the Traveller, in the style of the recently facelifted Mini and Beetle, and we'll be able to pop along to an air-conditioned showroom full of German imitation Travellers complete with fake quarterlights, power steering, electric windows and heaters which actually heat. And on the back there'll be a mock ash frame made of a polyurethane veneer that's practically impossible to tell apart from the original.

Good grief, I can't imagine anything worse. Truth is, on a sunny day, when she's not playing up, it's a joy to be out in

Milly. Whenever we park, someone will come up to us and recount some anecdote about someone they knew once owning one. We'll probably be driving Milly 'til our feet go through the floor or frostbite prevents us from operating the foot dip button. And if we end up selling her for scrap, well, at least we'll have some well-seasoned kindling.

Meeting your heroes

2012

Maybe it's the fact that I'll be turning fifty this month that I keep thinking about lost opportunities. For example, all the famous people I've had the chance to meet over the years, but didn't. The small number of celebs I *have* met in my humble half-century pale into insignificance when compared with the number I was basically too chicken to go up and talk to. And now, as I clock up the big five-o, those lost opportunities seem to be really getting to me.

I remember being in the small back room of a pub in Marylebone one Sunday afternoon in the eighties and it turned out the place belonged to Georgie Best. As the afternoon progressed, I realised through the thick fug of smoke and alcohol, that there was the man himself, leaning against a wall, chatting amiably to people over on the other side of the pool table. Now George was by far my biggest sporting hero as a young child. I had no interest in any of his off-field shenanigans; all I cared about was the blinding skill, the charisma. He lit up my world. Here was my opportunity to stroll over and shake the man by the hand. It was a pleasant enough atmosphere. There weren't even that many people in there. George looked right at me at one point. It would have been so easy. Then I could say, "I shook Georgie Best's hand!"

But I didn't. I don't know why. Something to do with not wanting to bother him, probably. Experience has taught me that in a situation like this you do have to have something prepared. You don't want to be remembering the time you met your hero being an awkward moment when you shook their hand and then stared blankly at them. Anyway, the opportunity slipped away.

Another time I was walking down the street in London's West End one evening and a man in a doorway stopped me and said, "Here mate, we're making a video with Paul McCartney and we need a few more people to be standing around. Want to be in it?" Guess what I did. I thought to myself, Nah, I always preferred the Stones to the Beatles. Which is still true, but still stupid, stupid, stupid. Now, at fifty, I look back at that day as the day I threw away a) the chance to be in a Paul McCartney video, and b) the chance to meet arguably the greatest living British pop star.

I could go on. But it's too depressing. I'm sure we've all got such stories. Well, all us fully paid-up members of the 'Life's Spineless Onlookers Club' anyway.

In 1953, my dad had an experience in London too. He was having a drink with an RAF pal in the bar of a swanky hotel. They were stunned when they realised that their idol, John Wayne, was sitting at the bar, drinking whisky. After much deliberation, Father gingerly walked up to the great man and said, "Excuse me, Mr. Wayne. I just wanted to say I've seen all your films and I think you're the greatest". My dad was nineteen, just a boy from Truro doing National Service, on a night out in the big city. And do you know what John Wayne said to him? He turned slowly, looked at the teenager, smiled, and said, "Well, gee, son. That sure is nice of you to say so". John Wayne said that to my dad! It sends shivers up my spine just thinking about it. Father certainly had no regrets about that little encounter. Recalling that story gave him such pleasure right up to the day he died. Now that's the way to do it.

Anyway, now that I'm practically fifty I've decided it's all going to change. Carpe Diem. You never regret the things you do in life, only the things you don't do. You may never get the chance to meet your heroes, but if you ever do, grab it, because it's not going to happen again.

Now, where was it that I saw Jenny Agutter...

Sense of direction

2013

I have a confession. As a chap, it takes a lot for me to admit this. It might seem ridiculous, but I've got a terrible sense of direction.

I don't mean 'ridiculous' because I'm a chap, and we're better at finding our way round than the ladies. Certainly not. The fact is, I was born in Redruth, of fairly intact Cornish ancestry. I know certain lanes and B roads pretty well. But I go into a sort of panic mode at the thought of anything less familiar. My brain becomes scrambled with a gallery of indistinct memories of places I've been to once or twice, and which lane they were down, off which road. It all gets a bit, well, muzzy. It's very similar to the feeling you get when you're at a party and someone starts talking to you, and you know that you should know their name. And they know that you should know their name. But because of all these expectations, your mind goes blank for a second, and after that you panic, and you'll never remember the name now. Until the person walks away, you relax, and you remember the name straightaway.

I'm OK with the basic stuff. Falmouth to Redruth, no problem. And I can do slightly trickier, say Perranporth to St Austell (mainly because it would involve the A30. Funny how that ghastly highway can be a sort of comfort sometimes). But ask me to get from, oh I don't know, say, Par to Mawgan Porth, then it's rabbit in the headlights time. I'm all, 'Well, I suppose I'll go back through St Austell, but I'm sure it would be more direct to go through, er, Roche, is it, but I've no idea where the turning is, and anyway the bigger roads are usually quicker even if they're further, so sometimes it can be a false economy...' And if you put me anywhere near one of those inconvenient little rivers, like the Helford, or the Fowey, I'm almost literally all at sea.

When we moved into my cottage twelve years ago, I put a big map of Cornwall on the wall of a certain small room I use several times a day, in order that I could regularly drum Cornish geography into my little brain. But it hasn't worked. I just don't have the attention span. I find I'm much more interested in trying to find the funniest place names. My current favourite is Greensplat. Followed by Crimp.

This definitely explains why I so love walking the coast path. True, it veers madly away from the coast at times, and if you're in West Penwith when a sea mist rolls in and you're wearing down your fingernails clambering over those granite outcrops, you might as well be lost on Dartmoor. But usually it's straightforward. It's obvious that if you're on the north coast and you're walking towards Lands End, you ensure that the sea is on your right and you can't go too far wrong. Hang on. Or is it left.

Thinking about it, my sense of direction used to be a lot better. But since I acquired a certain route-mapping device, I've just stopped bothering. Whatever caveman-based directional responsibility I may have once had has now disappeared for good. I've now let that part of my brain deteriorate to the extent that without this useful aid, I'd never find my way from my house to the end of the drive. I now take this failsafe device with me whenever possible. My wife. I know, it's crazy. No, not because she's a woman. I thought we'd already covered that. No, it's crazy because I'm eight years older than her, and I've spent twenty more years in Cornwall. Yet if we want to get from A to B, she'll work out the route quicker than me every time. And so I've given up trying. If only she'd let me have a little go on my own once in a while, maybe I'd still stand a chance.

Ah well. It could be worse. You should see my profiteroles. They're way better than hers.

Pushing the limits

2005

L ast month I was in Switzerland. One particular day my wife and I found ourselves strolling along a lakeside avenue in the pretty town of Montreaux, right on the Lake Geneva shoreline. Like Hillary and Sherpa Tenzing ascending the southern face in '53 we were trussed-up in multiple layers of thermal fleecy insulation with only our eyes and noses available to abuse from the sub-zero elements. These sorts of conditions are quite scary to an English person, let alone a Cornish one, as it just doesn't get this cold back home. The British tourist in this situation tends to do his sightseeing in a bit of a hurry, with the constant promise of a nearby hotel or café, with its sweltering underfloor heating, its locals sitting around in short-sleeved shirts, and its damnably tempting *chocolat chaud*.

As we walked, I started feeling quite disorientated. I was noticing things that didn't belong in this sub-zero landscape at all. Plants I was used to seeing at Heligan, or Tresco Abbey Gardens, were all happily growing by the side of the path, looking lovely, and, as far as I could tell, quite at home. There were phormiums, and ferns. There were chusan palms, and acacias. There were fatsias and yuccas. Yet it was freezing. Below freezing. Surely this wasn't right. I checked that the nearest phormium wasn't plastic. It wasn't. Its leaves felt pretty blooming cold, but it was real. Then I looked into the distance and realised that the hillsides was covered in grapevines. Grapevines! There were tens of thousands of them, all standing in a foot of snow, like beleaguered infantrymen at Vimy Ridge, dreaming of somewhere warmer. This was Switzerland, for goodness sake. A country synonymous with snow, mountains, cuckoo clocks, snow, skiing, and snow. Just what exactly was all this southern-hemisphere, sub-tropical, sexy, botanical exotica doing here? I mean, wasn't it a bit *chilly*?

Back home in Cornwall I found myself paying particular attention to people's gardens. And I got to thinking, you know, we British have a lot in common with those optimistic Swiss. Plant-wise anyway. The fact is that despite their exotic looks, those plants I saw in Switzerland were hardy. At least, hardy enough to survive in the specific location into which each one had been placed. The very essence of gardening for many of us is to cultivate whatever plants we possibly can within the boundaries of our own circumstances and ability. Those phormiums didn't belong in Switzerland any more than those stunning echiums belong along the seafront in Penzance, but if they can happily survive in these locations, then why not? It seems strange to use the sort of parlance usually reserved for the more obvious adrenaline sports like surfing and nude bungee jumping, but, in our modest and unassuming way, we gardeners are always 'pushing the limits'.

In Cornwall, the 'garden capital of Europe' as I've heard it described recently, we're an extreme example of this

197

phenomenon. Thanks to the gulf stream the whole country's maritime climate is pleasantly mild considering our latitude (spend a winter in Newfoundland for a good comparison), but down here in Cornwall it's even better. People grow the most amazing plants outdoors here. We love it. Who can fail to be impressed by a display of puyas, echevarias and agaves?

Just look at the new garden down at the Minack Theatre. When I first saw it I couldn't quite believe such tender-looking succulents could survive in this exposed spot. But of course, this classic Cornish location is what most of these plants love: tons of light, salty winds, and not much in the way of nutrients. The truth is that many so-called exotics are quite easy to grow. Think of all those beautiful alpine plants thriving on screes, thousands of feet above sea level. Look at the sexy yucca, originating from the deserts of America, where poor soil and cold night temperatures are what it wants. It's a common misconception that an exotic-looking plant will only thrive somewhere unremittingly hot.

It's when we gardeners push a plant beyond its limit that we get into the world of mulching, cutting-back and dragging things in from the garden every autumn in order to protect it over the cold winter months, just so it can be dragged outside again to impress our friends come May. If you took an aerial photograph of a suburban housing estate on a fresh October Sunday afternoon, I reckon every other back garden would feature a hunched figure dragging a reluctant tree fern or bottlebrush, complete with half ton pot, into the greenhouse. It's traditional.

If you ask me this is going a bit far, and thankfully in Cornwall there's less of this sort of caper going on. Who cares if you can get your cannas to flower a few days earlier by overwintering them indoors? I like to place plants where they belong, for good. If I get it wrong, they may perish. It's not like it's a dog.

Pasty pastry

2006

I knew it would happen. I held off mentioning the word 'pasty' in this magazine for three and a half years, for fear of provoking a hornet's nest situation. Then in August I threw caution to the wind and attempted to discuss the subject of pasty ingredients. All hell broke loose. Talk about a controversial subject. Talk about a bulging postbag. The response to the previous three and a half years' worth of *Backalongs* put together couldn't equal the personal backlash and reactionary bile unleashed by my humble pasty piece. I'll certainly think twice before tackling such a controversial subject as pasties again.

Which brings me to the pastry. Every bit as tricky as the ingredient list, this, and every bit as contentious. Now as I'm just a middle-aged bloke, obviously I couldn't hope to be taken seriously as a credible maker of pastry. So I conducted a lengthy, detailed and exhaustive survey into the construction techniques of pasty pastry, utilising a panel of Cornish grandmothers, who are truly the only reliable source.

But I ended up in a right pickle. Their description of perfect pasty dough ranged from 'poor' to 'not short' to 'not short, but not too flaky either'. All the Cornish grannies in my survey make great pasties, but not one could be specific about the mixture. And that, I reckon, is the point. They just do it. They've been doing it so long they can't remember how. It's instinctive, like riding a bike. It reminds me of that story about the housewife who always cuts the legs off a chicken when she roasts it. A friend asks her why, and she replies, "My mother always used to." Her curiosity roused, the housewife asks her mother why she did it, and her mother replies, "My mother always used to." So the housewife asks her grandmother who replies, "My mother always used to." So the housewife asks her great grandmother, who replies, "I had a very small roasting pan..."

And then there's the crimping. Ah, that most venerated of all ye olde Cornish artes. It doesn't matter how great the pastry, if the crimping's not up to scratch the whole thing's a disaster. Ineffective crimping means a great ugly zawn appearing down the thing and its guts spilling out all over the place. Over zealous crimping and you end up with a hideous, doughy rope ruining the look of the thing and making you reach for the Milk of Magnesia before you've even sniffed it.

As for the positioning of the crimping, again, everyone has their own opinion, and they will defend it til they die. Side? Top? Three quarters? Does it matter to people? You bet it does. How well I remember a stand up argument that took place with ex-pat relatives in Canada when we all attempted to have an old-fashioned family pasty making afternoon. There we all were standing in a kitchen, flour in our hair, skidding on bits of slimy chopped onion, the hot air smeechier than a Newlyn smokehouse. As soon as we got to the crimping, any semblance of family decorum went out the window altogether. It was Crimp Wars. And, again, what does it really matter? Who knows what traditional crimping looked like anyway? There's that well-worn old theory trotted out to the tourists about the miners using the crust as a handle to hold with their dirty hands, and then throwing it away, but I can't find much evidence, either documented or anecdotal. I certainly can't imagine those desperate, impoverished folk two hundred years ago wasting food in any circumstances, no matter how grubby it was. Not when your average Cornish miner was used to living in one tiny room with his entire family, walking miles to work a twelve hour day down a dark hole, barely able to afford to light the candle to work by.

There certain aspects about pasty pastry upon which I'm sure we can all agree. A hole is necessary as a steam release valve, lest the whole thing should overheat inside. Also, this is vital for releasing the unmistakable aroma of the most divine, yet simple dish created by Man. And we agree that the pastry thickness must be a fine balance between thin enough to be appetising, and thick enough not to spring a leak. In my experience this is the greatest skill of all. But for me no home-made pasty ever seems quite right without my little pastry initial on it, just like my mum used to do, in order to differentiate between mine and my brother's. Mind you, this did once cause a look of consternation on the face of a new girlfriend from upcountry when I introduced her to proper pasties for the first time and confidently announced, "I have to have a pee on mine, otherwise it doesn't taste the same."

The Cornish Fool

2009

Nine years ago my wife and I were house hunting. As we viewed our cottage for the first time, we had all the obvious concerns (wobbly walls, whether a hypermarket was about to be built next door, whether any of the neighbours ran a 24-hour pneumatic drill repair shop...that sort of thing). As the vendors enthusiastically reeled off all the selling points, they said something about an old preacher who'd once lived there.

"And what was that about a preacher?" my wife said to me as we drove away.

"Dick something. Born there, I think he said," I replied. We didn't think much more about it at the time.

We bought the place, and they kindly left us with a little framed picture of this old preacher, a potted history of his family, and the name of an obscure, out-of-print Victorian book about him.

During the ensuing years, I looked into the house's past and the mysterious preacher. I even eventually found a man who had a copy of the elusive biography. Having digested its contents, my life had changed rather. This chap was a bit of a legend. His name was Richard Hampton, the Cornish Pilgrim Preacher. But people knew him as Foolish Dick.

Foolish Dick started life as the type of character you often encounter in literature and films. The social misfit, who, through no fault of his own, is castigated by society and mercilessly mocked for not fitting in. The hunchback Quasimodo, Lennie in *Of Mice and Men*, or John Mills' village idiot character for which he won an Oscar in *Ryan's Daughter*. They always have one thing in common: they are almost invariably likeable, sympathetic characters with hidden depths. Maybe it's the fact that they are often so cruelly victimised by their community, but they're the chap we root for. They're the one who makes us want to shout at the screen, "Hey, you ignorant villagers! Let him go! He's worth ten of you!"

Dick didn't have much going for him. Born in 1782 into the poverty of a west Cornwall mining family, he was strange-looking, with a peculiarly thick-set body, disproportionate limbs, a huge face and head, and an odd, shuffling gait. His eyes looked in different directions and flickered constantly, so it's easy to imagine how he would have been written off as a village idiot. But it seems there was something metaphysical about Foolish Dick's brain, enabling him to commit vast chunks of the bible to memory.

He ended up preaching throughout Cornwall, and beyond. He became famous, and people travelled from all over to hear him. A sort of confidence exuded from him, and he could hold his audience spellbound. Dick's thick-set body, strange twitches and comical eyes, all combined with such a powerful and authoritative delivery, gave him what was described as a 'weird power' over people.

He had a naughty side too. My favourite story is about the time he found himself sitting between two travellers from London, both keen to mock the apparent dimwit, asking him, "We want to know whether you are a rogue or a fool."

"Why," replied Dick, looking at one and then the other, "'tween the two, I reckon!"

Dick's family remained in the little terrace of three tiny, one-up-one-down miners' cottages until the beginning of the 20th century. Now, of course, this poignant birthplace of this fascinating Cornish character is home to an altogether less charismatic character. Foolish Pete.

How well I remember trying to stay awake in school history lessons, staring at those turgid textbooks, trying to cram those meaningless, dry dates into my reluctant brain. But history becomes real so quickly when your imagination is sparked into life by something more tangible. There have, of course, been other more famous Cornish preachers, so it might be a year or two before I open up the Foolish Dick Visitor Centre, Gift Shop and Theme Pub. But you never know. We come to appreciate things more as time goes by.

After all, it doesn't seem so long ago you were allowed to chip bits off Stonehenge.

Nest box camera

2010

L ast summer I was given a nest box camera for my birthday. The sort you rig up to your telly via a long lead, then watch things develop from the comfort of your armchair, just like on *Springwatch*. I'd always wanted one of these clever contraptions, so my boys could enjoy the wonder of nature unfolding before their eyes when they get a bit older. Surely watching a little nestful of blue tits must be as good as anything for teaching a youngster about the whole circle of life thing. Thus the boys would never grow up to be like those 12-year-olds you see on Channel 4 documentaries who can't recognise a dog. Actually I think it was a Jamie Oliver programme, and it was artichokes, but you get the point.

I got round to rigging the box up in early October. It was straightforward, once I'd worked out how to get an electric cable into a cottage with walls 3 feet thick. For weeks, every time I turned on the TV, I quickly checked the nest box to see if anything remotely avian had blessed it with a visit. My wife found it hilarious. "No! Nothing in there today!" I'd shout from the front room, to no-one in particular, as I stared forlornly at the empty, grey nest box floor on the TV screen. I don't know what I really expected at that time of year. Maybe a woodlouse.

After a month, I did actually see a woodlouse, clear as you like, doing clockwise circuits of the inside of the box. Simon King wouldn't have been any more enthusiastic if he'd spotted a pack of hyenas playing gin rummy. "A woodlouse!" I shrieked, ludicrously excited. "It works!"

"That's nice, dear," the missus replied from a distant room.

The rest of the year passed without incident. Every day I checked the TV, and every day the same depressing nest box floor. I started worrying that the boys would develop a spontaneous aversion to birdwatching in the future, because that cursed box was always the first thing to come onto the TV screen, and it would invariably delay them in their lust to watch *Peppa Pig*. And that, to a two-year-old, is a very bad thing indeed.

Christmas came, and our next door neighbour Paul was given a nest box. He put it up, and within an hour had lusty looking blue tits busily bobbing in and out, deciding if it was a des enough res. I didn't need this. "Oh how lovely," I said, as we watched the annoying little balls of fluff flitting in and out, secretly wondering why I hadn't seen so much as a beak poking through the little hole in mine after two months, and even considering a bit of far-from-festive sabotage involving a cork and some wood glue.

The big January freeze arrived, and there was much reporting in the news of what strange things small birds were doing to survive. Eighty-three wrens were apparently observed huddling in a nest box together to survive somewhere up north. I turned on the TV. Nothing. I'd have been grateful to see a couple of earwigs huddling for survival, never mind anything that tweeted.

The nesting season loomed. Nature waits for no-one. I told myself that it's a bit like when you go fishing. You wouldn't want to catch a fish straightaway, or you'd get blasé about it all. You need to suffer a bit for it, to work for it. But what was I doing wrong exactly? The box was the right height, facing the right way, with the right size hole. This was getting ridiculous. March came, and as the snowdrops faded, a sight I'd been dreading: the first rook carrying a beakful of twigs. By the beginning of April the annual nesting frenzy was well underway. Every nest box I gazed upon was feverish with activity. Except one.

And now June is here, the garden is alive with bird life, and…

Ah, but that would be telling.

Technofear

2011

T wenty years ago, I thought I was keeping up with technology quite well. I remember buying a CD player, and thinking it was pretty nifty. But things have rather sped up since then, technology wise, and now I feel like I'm drowning in a sea I don't understand. I don't resent the fact that we've all got mobiles and computers and Satnavs; it's just that whenever I try to join in, it never quite seems to work.

There are so many examples. Look at MP3 players (does anyone even know what that stands for?). My wife gave me one of these gizmos for Christmas, but apparently I need a new version of an operating system on my computer before I can even put any music onto the MP3 player. That version will cost twice as much as the MP3 player did in the first place. Funny, no-one mentioned that when she bought it. Then there are digital compact cameras. Sure, taking pictures with one is easy. But the same cannot be said of the baffling number of ways in which you can attempt to produce a photographic print from one.

Our telly was always a bit on the crackly side, but perfectly watchable. Now that it's all gone digital we lose channels for days or weeks at a time. I'm told I need to put a big aerial on the roof, or even a satellite dish, rather than the discreetly hidden one we've got in the attic, but I refuse to bolt such a carbuncle to the top of my pretty old cottage. How dare anyone instruct me to do such a thing?

I've had a mobile phone for a couple of years, and I'll admit it's been quite handy (mostly on trips to London, funnily enough, where there's a phone box on every street corner). But the thing doesn't seem to get a signal wherever I go in Cornwall. And anyway, now that I've got a mobile phone, I realise they aren't phones at all – these days they're internet-browsing, movie-making, lifestyle management systems. These things will rule your whole life if you let them. The mere thought of capitulating to such a machine fills me with dread.

One more thing. I keep hearing ads on the radio for all the wonderful new BBC digital radio stations. But I've noticed they keep quiet about the fact that you can't hear any of them without buying a special new kind of radio.

It's all just so complicated, this 21st century living. Am I the only person who feels this way? Am I that unusual? All this amazing new technology is fine if you want to play along with it. But it all seems like such hard work. You have to pay attention, you have to upgrade things, and change constantly, and buy more and more stuff to sustain it all.

I bought my record player in 1978 and it's never given me a moment's grief, despite being carted around at least a dozen flats and houses. Tekkies might laugh at me, but I don't think having to turn a record over is a huge inconvenience compared with the hoops everyone seems to be jumping through to keep up with technology these days. I would, genuinely, rather go back to a world with no mobiles, no HD, and just a handful of TV channels. And records you played on a record player. And rolls of film you took to Boots.

Of course, we now have a generation of young people for whom this 'enforced future' isn't frightening or alien at all; it's natural, and normal. It's desirable. A record player for them is as laughable as tweeting somebody is to me.

Thank goodness I've got three-year-old children. A ready made IT department. Sometime in the next few years I expect them to start running things around here. I just hope I can make it til then, because at the moment I'm disappearing into a black hole of technofear.

Plastic chough decoy

2010

We're all obsessed with something. With me, as you may know, it's choughs. The novelty and wonder of our sacred birds returning to Cornwall is showing no sign of abating as far as I'm concerned, even as we near (I can hardly believe it), the *tenth anniversary* of their return to Cornwall. Yes, those three wild choughs showed up here way back in 2001, and their offspring have been slowly but steadily colonising our coastline ever since.

This year there were three successful nests, with several more potential parents practising nest-building for next year. Three nests may not sound a lot, but it's an awful lot more than none at all, which is what I'd thought we'd have to endure for ever more. For this Cornishman, there may as well be a thousand nests.

But it is because the chough's return has been so successful that my obsession has taken a slightly different tack of late. It was OK when we only had choughs down on the Lizard. They were the '*Lizard choughs*'. But after a few years, various choughs started to spread their wings and make forays further west. Pretty soon they were around Land's End. This was great, of course, but the reality was that they weren't the '*Lizard choughs*' any more. And then it hit me: the very real, and utterly intoxicating possibility that a chough could one day fly over my house.

I live on the coast about half way between Hayle and Newquay, so theoretically once a chough with itchy wings decides the grass is greener on this side of St Ives Bay, well, it could be stopping by anytime. To hope for such a thing is a modest ambition, isn't it? Not some sad, unachievable goal, like a hankering for space travel, or Cornwall to have a majority of Lib Dem MPs again, or for my annual water bill to drop below £1,000. No, those would be silly.

I haven't been idle in facilitating my dream. Anyone who visits my house can't help noticing there's a tasteful plastic chough decoy nailed to the garage roof. It's been there eight years. Apart from the occasional low flypast by a passing rook it's been, frankly, a waste of time. It certainly hasn't justified my annual efforts on a stepladder, touching up its faded bill and legs with my little tin of scarlet model aircraft paint.

There have been plenty of false alarms along my bit of the coastline over the years. Unreliable sightings, by deluded optimists like me, giving the occasional backlit crow with a slightly dusty beak the benefit of the doubt and phoning the RSPB with an exultant but bogus chough sighting. In November last year a temporary postman in the village reckoned he'd seen three nearby. No-one else did.

But it all changed in April this year, with a reliable sighting of two choughs at Hell's Mouth, heading for Portreath. I could hardly believe it. This was it. They'd done it. They'd crossed the bay. Next, a sighting at Chapel Porth, and then Penhale, the other side of Perranporth. If this was true, they'd flown past my house, and I hadn't even noticed. This wasn't supposed to happen! I'd always assumed they'd have the decency to let me know. You know, after all I'd done for them. I felt spurned, like when an old friend reveals they were in Cornwall last year staying in a B&B down the road but didn't bother popping in. Come to think of it, that sort of thing seems to be happening to me more frequently these days. I can't imagine why.

Us north coast choughy-obsessives have been out there looking for the elusive pair all year. We know they're out there, cruising up and down the north coast. Plenty have seen them, but so far they've eluded me. I'm not giving up though. This is just too exciting.

Now, where did I put that red paint?

Surfing:
you just can't fake it

2004

W hy on earth is it called 'Surfing the net'? What possible similarity can there be between looking up information on a computer screen, and the most adrenalin-pumping thrill in the world? I've never been able to work that one out.

A while back I watched that TV programme where they take someone from a completely inappropriate walk of life and try to turn them into something they are not. In this one they took a twenty-something desk-bound London computer nerd and tried to turn him into a surfer competent enough to enter a competition and not get spotted as a fake, inside a month. An analogy was made about him going from surfing the net to surfing the waves. Very funny. They brought him from London and set him up in St Agnes, introducing him to two local surf gurus. They bleached his hair. They clad him in cool beach wear. They gave him a fake tan. They hired an acting coach to give him confidence. Oh, and they taught him to surf.

As the month went by, the amiable guinea pig tried his hardest. He learned the lingo, swore a lot, and got browner and more weatherbeaten by the day. By the end he was loving the whole lifestyle, promising that on returning to London he was going to change his life because he now loathed the way he used to be. The change in him was a pleasure to watch. But what about the contest at the end of the month? Did he fool the judges? Of course not. He could barely stand up.

The truth about surfing is that it is very hard. It takes absolute dedication for a sustained period, as well as a generous helping of natural ability, to get seriously good. Surfers, real ones, are in the water every day, conditions permitting. It takes over their life. Go to any Cornish beach when the waves are half decent, on any day of the year during daylight hours, and you'll see them out there. Putting the hours in. It involves a unique blend of physical fitness, stamina, agility, balance, wave-judgment and sheer bravery. These people are athletes. Really serious surfers are paying close attention to things like meteorology and nutrition too. Unfortunately the aspiring professional surfer has a major PR problem compared with, say, the average aspiring Olympic swimmer. Whereas the life of the latter is usually portrayed as an endless drudge of pre-dawn training sessions at a depressing local leisure centre and tedious exercising, the surfer is usually spotted on or near a beach, or in the sea, laughing frequently. The surfer isn't working any less. He's just having a lot more fun.

And I should know. I've failed at surfing, on and off, for the past thirty years. I know how hard it is. At 19 I did get good enough to realise what all the fuss is about. I can honestly say that nothing I have ever done can quite compare to the sensation of plummeting down the face of a six foot wave, feet barely in contact with the board, leaning into your bottom turn, making it, and feeling your fingertips throwing a clean fan of translucent spray out behind you as they briefly slice through the sheer green face of pure ocean energy that's racing past you. But I moved away from the sea for too long, and got too fat, and now when I go in the water I'm well out of my comfort zone. So I find myself standing on the beach in awe, constantly flirting with the idea of getting back in the water, but rarely making it.

The truth is that riding a wave is a rush the like of which cannot be found anywhere else. It's not surprising that once people tap into it, they never get over it. Cornwall is increasingly full of people who have given their lives over to the pursuit of the perfect wave. It may sound like an old hippy cliché, but it really isn't far short of a religion. Like the innocent abducted into a questionable cult, surfers can be seduced into a lifestyle where the wave rules their life. Generally speaking, if a surfer has food, shelter and, most importantly, access to a range of good breaks for different conditions, he's happy. A vehicle with petrol in it to get him further down the coast when one beach isn't working is about the most important luxury.

This obsession has of course been cynically expoited by a thousand T-shirt companies extolling the virtues of living the dream and, beyond that, created a multi-million dollar industry that is 'surf wear'. The problem is that unfortunately these days it's only these trappings of surfing that we see. Surfing's a victim of its own success. The lifestyle and fashion aspect is so appealing to us that it dominates the sublime experience that surfing is. It seemed absurd years ago when surf shops started opening in Cornish towns miles from the sea. "Who's going to buy a surfboard in Truro, for goodness sake?" we asked ourselves. But we were missing the point. Now you get them in Covent Garden. Damien Hirst is using longboards as an art medium. It matters not whether you've ever even got your toes wet, people just want to identify with the lifestyle. It's as if the makers of that TV show assumed that if the lad was appropriately immersed in the paraphernalia then actually riding a wave would be of secondary importance. But streaky hair and a £40 T shirt do not a surfer make. It's absurd to hope that a complete novice who has barely ever been in the sea could become an expert within a month. I wonder if the programme makers would have considered taking a man who's never hit a golf ball and giving him a month of lessons before competing in The Open. "Give him a Pringle tanktop and a BMW and no one will notice that he took 23 shots on the first."

In Cornwall we've seen surfing grow from a relatively obscure, under-appreciated fringe sport in the sixties and seventies, into a whole lifestyle which everyone seems to want to buy into. When Brits are sufficiently seduced by surfing's all-encompassing charms, then Cornwall is the natural place to head. We provide a neat microcosm of this international phenomenon, and it's the closest you're going to get to Hawaii, both geographically and spiritually, on our shores. Just visit the big summer contest at Fistral, Newquay if you require further proof. You won't be disappointed. The chap on the TV show was thus seduced. Although he achieved a lot in a month, the important thing was the change in him. The natural, non-materialistic lifestyle of his new buddies had changed him. Having dismally failed to convince any of the judges that he was a surfer, he didn't care. He'd got the message. He'd got a sniff of it and he wanted in.

He'd definitely opted for the more interesting type of surfing.

Being Cornish

2005

T he other day I was standing at a bus stop, conducting an experiment. Every time a bus approached, I'd ask the person next to me a question. "Where's the bus to?" I'd say. And the answer would tell me quite a lot. Allow me to explain.

I'd been listening to the lunchtime radio phone-in, and it was getting pretty heated. They were talking about what it takes for a person to be considered 'proper Cornish'. There was the usual procession of extreme views. First, someone saying how you had to be able to prove that at least three generations of your family (on both sides) had been born here to qualify as Cornish. Then someone called in saying how he didn't understand why anyone would want to claim Cornish identity anyway, because we're inbred morons. This was immediately followed by a well-timed call from a woman who reinforced his point by saying, "I dunno how 'e can say the Cornish are stupid, cos without the Cornish there wouldn' be no steam, nor trains, nor 'lectric, nor television". Thankfully a break for the news stopped her short of claiming rap music, cholesterol-reducing margarine and Buddhism as Cornish achievements.

Obviously the whole debate's a load of rubbish. There are simply too many loopholes in the various theories. Let's look at the three basic claims to being proper Cornish:

1) To be Cornish you simply have to be born here. That one falls flat on its face as we recall again a number of extremely well-known Cornish icons, none of whom were actually born here (Alfred Wallis, Brenda Wootton, Terry Frost...).

2) To be Cornish you have to have pure Cornish ancestry going back many generations, regardless of where you now live. So an appropriate candidate for this one would be a 95-year-old man in Australia, whose parents emigrated to there from Illogan in 1910 and has never even heard of Cornwall, nor ever been anywhere near Europe. Again, a bit of a dubious one.

3) To be Cornish you have to be born here, *plus* have pure Cornish ancestry. I'm not sure just how far back in time you're supposed to go with this to define 'pure Cornish ancestry' since I presume your claim is negated if you discover a great grandmother who was born in Torbay because her mother travelled there from Cornwall once in 1873 and happened to go into labour. I doubt if there is anyone in the world who could claim to be Cornish under this definition. I know I'd personally have to hang my head, reluctantly conceding a grandfather who originated in the Midlands, even though he spent most of his life working as a Cornish gardener. Sorry, I mean *gardener in Cornwall*. Oh, the shame of it. But at least it's out in the open now. I can begin to rebuild my life.

So anyway, I was beginning to conclude that in order to claim true Cornishness you have to be from an endless line of ancestors, not a single one of whom has ever, *ever* set foot east of the Tamar. Strict, yes, but fair.

And that's how I came to be standing at the bus stop. I've dreamt up a failsafe test for Cornishness that I'd like to hold up to the world as the scientific standard. When you've asked, "Where is the bus to?" the person has a choice of two answers. If they reply, "It's just coming," you know they understood the question correctly, and that they belong here. They may have only been here a few years, or they may be from a five-hundred year bloodline of Cornish knockers, but you'll know that, crucially, they understand *our ways*. And that's what matters. If, however, they reply, "Falmouth" then you'll know you've rumbled a Cornish wannabe.

It's impressive that in this great place we call home, our moribund language has been brought back from extinction and given cardiopulmonary resuscitation by a handful of brave souls. All over the country, regional traditions, accents and colloquialisms are dwindling as we all rush, lemming-like, into a globalised, brave new world. So what's wrong with rejoicing in our uniqueness, in the fact that we're not just another English county, by retaining the odd colloquialism? It's the least we can do.

The overrated sea

2008

I t's been a year since my grandmother passed away. Nan was a mine of information, a disarming source of old school wisdom, and, until her eyesight failed her, a merciless scrabble opponent. Plus, having lived in Cornwall for 100 of her 101 years, she was a deadly weapon in any pub 'Who sitting around the table is the most Cornish?' debate.

Nan said something quietly under her breath to my wife and I, just a few months before she died. At the time I thought little of it. But the more I reflect upon it, the more interesting I'm realising it is, a year on.

We'd take her on drives, like you do with old people who can no longer walk very well. And in Cornwall, where do you go to look at the scenery? Why, to the coast, of course. So we drove to the coast, like we always did. We bought an ice cream. And looked at the view, like you do. Nan was quiet, as ever.

And then suddenly (bearing in mind that she was approaching her 101st birthday), she says, "The sea's overrated. I've always thought so." My wife and I looked at each other, smiling in disbelief at this seemingly ungrateful and ludicrous comment, not quite knowing whether to laugh it off or enquire as to what she meant. Overrated? The sea that has shaped our history for millennia? The very reason that two out of our top

223

three industries ever existed? The sea that created the coastal landscape that has become the envy of the world? The sea that has provided the creative inspiration for centuries of artists and writers? *Overrated*?

"What d'you mean, Nan?" we asked.

"Well, everyone always goes and stares at the sea in Cornwall. But there's nothin' much to see is there? Just a grey old expanse of nothin'. Give me a wood or a Cornish hedgerow anyday. Now that's somethin' worth looking at. So much more goin' on."

Now, after a year of thinking about it, I think she might have had a point. My grandmother was a Cornish gardener's wife. The sea, to someone born in 1906, represented a vast mass of icy cold greyness which did little more than steal human lives and extend the distance between us and our loved ones who'd gone away to fight wars on our behalf. It was infinitely less understood then, a place that gave us fish, and seaweed for the garden, and little else. In the early 1900s you could swim in the sea, if you could stand the cold, but there were no wetsuits, no surfboards, none of the paraphernalia we now take for granted to help us unlock it all.

Sure, a fledgling tourist industry was developing in the early 1900s, and the beach was becoming a more popular place to be in the summer. But it's easy to see why a wood was more enticing for a little girl back then. It was there all year round. It was a haven to play in, with its boundless and fascinating flora and fauna, its trees to climb and birds' nests to find. It was atmospheric, exhilarating, endlessly interesting, and accessible.

Nan's life was hard enough. Why would she want to make it harder by wasting time going to a place that is only really comfortable for a handful of days per year? If you think about it, no-one in their right mind used to build their house with a sea view. A sea view was the last thing you wanted, because with it came howling winds and rattling windows. Constant immersion in salt spray put paid to all but the toughest plants, and rotted wood. A nice sheltered valley, that was the thing. It's only in our comfy, all-mod-cons modern world that we can call a sea view desirable, let alone pay so much money for the privilege of having one.

By the time her 101st birthday came round, Nan wasn't up for a big celebration of the type we'd had for her hundredth. So we took her for a drive. It was a lovely August day, and we remembered what she'd said. So we headed away from the coast, and explored all the beautiful, sun-dappled, leafy lanes around where she grew up in Summercourt. She couldn't see it too well, but what she saw, she loved. She couldn't get enough of it. In the circumstances, it was the perfect 101st birthday. She never stopped talking about it, not until the day she died. We were so glad she'd been honest with us.

It can be good to look at something in a different light. Sometimes we just can't see the woods for the trees. Or in this case, the sea.

Nappy

2005

So, here we all are again, dealing with the madness that is summer in Cornwall. The longest day might be a distant memory, but we all know that summer proper arrives with a vengeance in August. And all over the county we Cornish sit at home, twitching every time the phone rings. Relatives you hoped you'd never see again, and friends you thought you'd lost touch with years ago will be picking up the phone with fully prepared, 'off the cuff' little speeches: "We haven't really booked a big holiday this year," they'll say. "So we thought we'd just take the car and see where we end up. Um, are you very busy, with, um, with visitors this August?" And fighting the urge to say something along the lines of "Hmm, let's see. Cornwall. August. Of course we're *!*/*!! busy with visitors!" we meekly capitulate with a terribly polite "I'm sure we've got the odd window. Just let me get the diary". We hate ourselves, but we all do it.

And as the years go by, and I get more bitter and resentful as each exploitative houseguest romps with abandon through the private space my wife and I used to call home, sprinkling sand from every orifice, I find I demand more in return. It's my way of dealing with it. The current minimum acceptable tradeoff is a bunch of flowers and at least two bottles of decent wine on arrival, plus at least one fairly posh meal out. Surely it's not too much too ask. Not for several hundred pounds' worth of holiday accommodation it bloody isn't.

But something just happened which has taken me to a whole new level of houseguest revulsion. Way back at the end of last summer they were staying, the couple and their new baby. All very nice. "Oh yes," I distinctly recall them proclaiming. "These disposables are fully compostable." I'm all for recycling and composting everything we can, and frankly when the alternative was them leaving a bagful of the rancid things festering in our garage 'til bin day (oh yes, that's happened before), well, the compost heap seemed like a pretty good option. That was ten months ago.

Now I'm fully aware that foul things lurk in compost heaps. Adders raise whole families in there. Not that adders are foul, because they are a rare and beautiful creature which we should all be privileged to find in our garden. But you wouldn't half jump if you suddenly encountered one as you plunged your fork into your compost heap on a hot summer's day. Damn it, I accidentally put my hand on a slow worm the other day and it took me an hour to get over it. Biggest one I've ever seen. A foot long if it was an inch. And you get rats too.

But when I went to inspect the heap this very afternoon, and marvelled at how nature had created this fine, black, nutrient-rich tilth, imagine my surprise as a small, padded, relatively white bit of plastic attached itself immovably to my fork prong. All in one piece it was, every bit as intact as the day, ten months ago, when it was peeled, stinking, from the baby's backside, and I'd gullibly agreed to chuck it in the compost. It was so intact I reckon I could give it a rinse and return it to its rightful owner, on their inevitable arrival this coming August. Just to make a point. "How's that for recycling," I'd say.

And then I found another. And another, and another. Every cubic foot of my beautiful black horticultural gold appeared to be harbouring a little white surprise.

What kind of leaving present was this? Who in their right mind would treat their welcoming host this way? Either they knew at the time that their nappies weren't recyclable, in which case this was just some lazy way of getting rid of them without feeling too guilty, or else they genuinely believed them to be biodegradable and presumably have been liberally peppering the landscape with the things during the past ten months. Either way, I'm not very impressed.

Now I'm fully aware that all new parents display some morbid fascination with the exact contents of their darling progeny's diaper. It seems to be part of the bonding process or something. But why in heaven's name should they involve me like this? I'm not naming any names, but they know who they are. All I'm saying is, this coming August when they reappear on our well-trodden doorstep, the stakes will be raised, and they've only themselves to blame. At least four bottles of Camel Valley Bacchus, and dinner at The Black Pig. That's the deal. Enough said.

A Cornishman returns

2010

I realised the other day that I think I'm finally Cornish again. It's taken a few years, but I really feel I'm there now. For a start, I think I've got my accent back.

Years ago when I moved up to London, I'm ashamed to say I deliberately suppressed it. I can only think it was a sad, misguided and ultimately fruitless attempt to fit in with the posher upcountry types with whom I found myself sharing an office, and all of whom ironically found my Cornishness extremely endearing. My accent faded to a shadow of its former self, and by the time I finally had the sense to come back home (wife in tow), it had dwindled to a boring, generic sort of English version in which one might occasionally discern a very slight rolling of an 'r' in words like *'brother'* or lengthening of the 'a' in *'bath'*. I don't know how I let it happen, looking back.

Am I the only Cornish person to have behaved in this ridiculous way? A Cornish accent is a rare thing indeed these days. It should be treasured, not concealed. There are people out there on the front line trying to revive our language, for goodness sake. So surely just keeping the accent alive in an age when our teenagers talk like retarded Californians would be an achievement in itself?

We also have to keep our Cornish accents alive just to make a stand against their increasingly absurd portrayal in the media. Television has a lot to answer for here, going right back to some truly dreadful accents in Poldark in the seventies. Someone really should have had a word with the actor who played the doctor, Dwight Enys. Any rudimentary study of the way the Cornish pronounce the name 'Ross' will reveal that it is pronounced with a deep, throaty, 'o' vowel, and not a ridiculous, *Archers*-style, yokelly, 'Raaass'.

But things don't seem to have improved much since then. In fact they may even have got worse. Now, I realise I've moaned about this before, but the obvious culprit at the moment is that most surreal of TV shows, Doc Martin. That's the one in which a hemophobic London surgeon joins a community of Bristolians all living and working in a cluster of houses with enviable views of a Cornish harbour. Now I have no objection to the portrayal of us Cornish as quirky and charming, but the supporting characters of this programme all seem to be quirky and *stupid*. I'm sure that the show doesn't necessarily claim to represent Cornwall, but it is blatantly set here, so surely people upcountry are getting the subliminal impression that Cornish villages are full of idiots with peculiar accents.

I suppose I'm a bit bitter because the show's synopsis so strongly resembles that of my all-time favourite TV show, Northern Exposure (fish-out-of-water, overqualified city doctor arrives against his wishes in rural backwater, copes with quirky but endearing locals and battles with awkward receptionist in run-down surgery, reluctantly acknowledging

230

feelings for pretty but opinionated local teacher/bush pilot with whom he strikes up a hilarious will-they-won't-they, love/hate relationship).

I digress. So how is it that I'm so confident that I've got my Cornish identity back? Well, apart from the fact that I've definitely noticed myself rolling my 'r's again, I went on a rare visit to London recently. I was in the centre of town, and went into a shop to ask for directions. As I thanked the assistant, I found myself quite naturally doing a Cornish farmer's thumbs up. You know the one; when you clench your fist really hard, but leave your thumb protruding so very slightly that only the thumbnail is really visible. To those who know, it unambiguously signifies a Cornishman saying, 'Right on boy'. The stylish girl behind the counter looked at me and smiled sweetly. I realised what I'd done, and through my blushes the significance of the event dawned on me.

And I was so, so proud.

Taboo adjectives

2009

There are two adjectives you'll seldom hear coming from a Cornishperson's lips.

One is the word 'clotted', when applied to cream. I spent my entire childhood thinking there was only one sort of cream, never dreaming there could exist in the world any type other than the one you could stand a spoon up in, with a lovely yellow crust, which makes you sick if you eat more than half a tub of it on strawberries (ask my brother - hasn't touched the stuff since), and is most famously made in Scorrier by a company previously known as Wheal Rose Dairies, but now rhymes with Podda's. This divine, yet undeniably artery-clogging, teatime treat is, of course, known to the rest of the world as 'clotted' cream. That's clotted as in *thickened*. Only when I traversed the Tamar as a student did the existence of other cream types become apparent to me. In the college canteen in Bath I was offered cream on my apple pie, and the dinner lady proceeded to pour what appeared to be top-of-the-milk all over it. "What's that?!" I screeched, assuming she'd made a mistake. "You did say yes to cream, didn't you?" the bewildered woman replied.

And thus it began to slowly dawn on me. There's proper cream, which is clotted, and there's 'upcountry' cream, which can be 'single' (i.e. milky), or 'double' (i.e. not quite as milky). It takes a bit of getting used to for a Cornish boy. Since that occasion in the college canteen I've been in countless situations when I've had to reluctantly use that embarrassing adjective, 'clotted', in order to differentiate between real cream and that awful milky stuff.

The other taboo adjective is the word 'Cornish'. When applied to 'pasty'. This one's a bit more controversial. The only time the word 'pasty' is prefixed with the word 'Cornish' is when it's used by a visitor. Or someone upcountry. In fact when you order a pasty in a Cornish bakery, you don't even use the word 'pasty', let alone 'Cornish'. "Large steak please," suffices nicely. No need for extraneous information. Go into Rowes in Redruth and ask for a "Large steak Cornish pasty" and you'll look a bit of a twit. Down here, a pasty is *Cornish*, by definition, just as cream is *clotted*. If someone offered me a Cornish pasty I'd be very suspicious. Any Cornishperson would. I'd assume it didn't have much to do with Cornwall.

Yet oddly, there's an organisation called the Cornish Pasty Association, who aim to 'protect the quality and the reputation of the Cornish pasty and to stop consumers being misled by pasty makers who trade off the value of the name without producing a genuine product'. A pasty, say the CPA, must be made this side of the Tamar, and must contain those sacred four ingredients people always drone on about.

Well, I've heard it all now. The Pasty Police. It's like something out of Kafka. No, more like Reginald Perrin. Does this mean a 70-year-old Cornish grandmother living in

Plymouth would produce a less worthy pasty than an industrial unit on the A30 whose lorries transport their product by the thousand to service stations all over Britain, each with a little corporate sticker saying 'Genuine Cornish Pasty' on it? Call me old-fashioned, but I think I know which would be likely to taste nicer.

Just imagine the headlines if this strangeness had been going on a hundred years ago: 'Penniless Cornish fishwife condemned by Pasty Police for putting a bit of pilchard in her family's pasties instead of designated 'minced or roughly cut chunks of beef (not less than 12.5%)''. Or possibly, 'Farm workers castigated by society for using parsnip because they'd run out of turnip'.

Adjectives can be useful things though. In fact there's one word that should always be prefixed with the word 'Cornish'. Chough. Oh yes, those two go very nicely together.

Back to that nest box camera

2011

Y ou may remember last year in this column reading the sorry tale of my nest box camera. Despite taking great care to rig the thing up correctly, the only wildlife spectacle I ever saw on my TV screen was a lone woodlouse. And even the woodlouse looked as if he was just passing through on the way to somewhere more interesting. By the end of the nesting season I had absolutely no evidence that any bird had ever set foot in what seemed to me to be the perfect five star starter home. There was no getting away from it. I'd failed. They never seem to have such problems on *Springwatch*.

But that was then. This year everything changed. I'd noticed a great tit roosting in the box over the winter, which was exciting enough. And then in March, there were the unmistakable signs of nest-building: little bits of moss and feathers all over the nest box floor, which within days had turned into something positively luxuriant. Then it all happened so fast. BAM. An egg appeared. Then another. Next time I looked, seven perfect white eggs. Unbelievably perfect, just sitting there, huddled together, looking quite unreal. I watched, every day. This was too easy. Then chicks. First a hideous, writhing pile of flappy, bald, gaping, scrawny, baby dinosaurs, which became sweet balls of fluff, then, after little more than a fortnight, perfect little juvenile fledglings flying directly from the nest box to my feeder, right outside the kitchen window. One little one didn't make it, but I'm fairly confident the rest did.

Then a bonus. The box was empty, and I didn't bother checking it for a few days. Suddenly there were more eggs. I couldn't believe my eyes. A second brood. By this time the camera had been knocked out of place, and I could only see half the nest, but there were at least another five eggs, and five more chicks, going right into June. My nest box camera, that white elephant of a birthday present, and for a year the most depressing waste of time, had borne witness to the introduction of at least ten new great tits to the world. And I'd watched the whole thing on TV with my three-year-olds. Best birthday present I've ever had.

I've been trying to look objectively at what went wrong last year. All spring and summer there'd been birds hopping in and out of nest boxes all over my garden, yet the one with the camera in remained vacant. I'd ensured the hole was the regulation blue tit aperture size of 25mm, so surely even the most wily of titmice should have had the decency to take a sniff. I'd have settled for a slightly runty blue tit. Maybe they were simply suspicious of all that gadgetry. I mean, it's an intimate thing for a bird, isn't it, nesting? Most people wouldn't want a camera looming over their bed, filming everything that goes on, would they? OK, best not go there.

Looking back I think maybe I just overdid things. Like the neurotic newcomer to the estate, enthusiastically inviting their new neighbours round for drinks but trying much too hard to impress, scaring them off with forced conversation, and a carpet that's intimidatingly clean, and dauntingly perfect canapés, when all a guest wants is to feel comfortable. Maybe that was me. All my other nest boxes are scruffy affairs, made with rubbishy scraps of wood, and battered by years of abuse. This one was a thing of beauty. It had everything but a welcome mat. Never had I taken such care. I'd countersunk the screwholes, for heaven's sake. Perhaps the birds don't want that. Perhaps they pick up on it. Perhaps the thing just took a year to bed in, and grow a bit of lichen.

But I guess the most obvious conclusion here is patience. Good things come to those who wait. Now it's winter again, and my little friend is back in there roosting. I can't wait to see what happens next.

Fitting in II: Clothes

2010

Regular readers may remember a controversial column I wrote a few months back, in which I attempted to help an incomer friend feel at home here. I did this by suggesting he never wear shorts in winter, because a) it's silly and b) everyone will know he's only just moved here. My comments provoked quite a response, so I'd like to take this opportunity to step it up a notch and make a couple of further suggestions to aid assimilation into our Cornish ways. Just a couple more friendly do's and don'ts, based on a 47-year study.

For a start, anything involving pastel shades, especially with Breton fisherman's stripes, and often displayed on a loose-fitting rugby-style shirt, usually with the collar turned rakishly up, is a dead giveaway. Dress like this and you'll instantly brand yourself a second homeowner trying a bit too hard. That is unless you are extremely confident, and own an actual yacht, in which case you could get away with it. You do see a lot of this sort of thing in St Mawes. If you want to have a go at creating this image you need to rigorously back comb your hair for that 'Just sailed back from Scilly' look.

We often get catalogues through the letterbox by manufacturers of this type of clobber. Such publications invariably feature improbably youthful, sixty-something, white-haired models, laughing with abandon as they ride funky-looking bicycles with their feet off the pedals, pastel jumpers thrown casually over their shoulders, then posing with their equally gorgeously-tanned children and grand-children for a stroll across a deserted, windswept beach. With their trousers rolled up. Holding hands. Always photographed on a tilt.

Oh yes, I've seen them.

Don't get me wrong though; one must dress casually at all times if one wants to blend in here in Cornwall. But you want to get it right. You can't go wrong with navy blue, especially when it's authentically sun/wind bleached. This is a look you don't get from a catalogue. The retired incoming gentleman might even wish to consider that iconic classic, the peaked fisherman's cap, in navy or black, bestowing as it does instant credibility upon its wearer, assuming it's adequately faded. This effect can also be achieved by hanging it outside on the clothes line for a couple of years before wearing.

You could try designer surf gear of course, but if you ask me most people fail miserably at this look. Anyway, I've never really got to grips with the strange paradox of this particular fashion. On one hand you've got the natural rush of riding a wave, and on the other you're expected to embrace an apparently unrelated fashion niche which forces you to spend a fortune on a ridiculous T-shirt featuring sophisticated, urban typography, deemed by somebody to be this year's 'must have'. But then I suppose I'm coming at it from the perspective of a seventies surfer/skateboarder for whom a proper surf T will always feature Gerry Lopez riding the Banzai Pipeline backlit by an orange, stripy sunset, all framed by the feathery fronds of a tropical palm tree. I distinctly remember having one in lemon yellow. With a nice sensible front pocket for my Opal Fruits.

Which brings me to sunglasses. Only when the sun's out, please. That's kind of the point. Never on the top of your head, round the back of your head, clamped to your neck, or when indoors, drizzling, or night. I know this sounds obvious, but you'd be surprised.

Wait a minute. I seem to have run out of space. But I've only just started. Maybe this handy style guide will have to become a little series.

One last thing though: ponytails on men. Good grief, talk about trying too hard.

Just like Axel

2009

My children's book has been out almost two years now. Obviously I might have to wait another year or two for it to achieve the cult status of, say, *Jonathan Livingston Seagull* or *The Gruffalo*, but Rome wasn't built in a day.

Actually I've got mixed feelings about *The Gruffalo* anyway, because I went to art college with the man who drew him, Axel Scheffler. It was obvious that Axel was destined for great things, because he was so dedicated, not to mention the only one to get a first class degree. Plus, he's German. This meant that he actually spent his college years working, unlike us more traditional, layabout-type students of the kind so prevalent in the early eighties, unencumbered as we were by today's loathsome student loan culture, let alone such scary and alien words as 'vocation' and 'career'.

Axel was plainly talented from day one. But when one looks at a contemporary who's gone on to achieve success, one can't help thinking, to some extent: *'It could have been me. If only I'd had the ability, inclination, determination, originality, contacts, tenacity, ambition, and the moon had been in Aries when they dished out the degrees, it could have been me.'*

But I like to think my book's making slow but steady progress in the bookshops. It's even won an award. A real one.

Other highlights so far have included doing a signing at Truro's *Waterstones* during which they sold so many books that they ran out. Oh, and getting good reviews from proper, bona-fide, respectable celebrity critics such as the BBC's Chris Packham and Neil Oliver, to whom I'll be eternally grateful (you can't be afraid to name-drop in this game).

Of course if I was more dedicated and hardworking, like Axel, I'd have embarked on a national promotional tour of schools, leaving no stone unturned in the pursuit of book sales. But I never seem to find the time, nor the self-confidence. Perhaps one day. I have done the odd school visit, and enjoyed them, by and large. They can be a bit of a revelation. There you are, trying to enthuse a bunch of apparently disinterested 11-year-olds about your book and the choughs therein, when someone puts their hand up and asks, "Why do crows go 'kraarrk!' and choughs go 'cheow!'?" They might as well kick the chair out from under you. They keep you on your toes, kids do.

Another time, I visited a rural school in west Cornwall and a rosy-cheeked boy at the back finally plucked up the courage to mumble, "Your book. 'ow many tractors has it got in it?" Slightly embarrassed, I politely replied, "Oh, well, actually, I don't think there are any tractors in it at all, I'm afraid. Sorry about that; perhaps I'll make sure I include a tractor or two in my next book. OK?" The boy didn't reply. He just looked at me, blankly, and then said, quietly, "No. Chapters." We all shuffled uncomfortably. I tried to laugh it off: "Did I mention it's won an award?" I probably said.

But unquestionably the biggest highlight of being published is the fact that you can, in some small way, affect people. I'm perfectly happy to accept that my book won't affect most people's lives at all, but when you receive a single comment from a ten-year-old girl, who looks you in the eye and says, "It's the best book I've ever read," and her parents say, "It's true. She finished it and started reading it again straightaway," it really doesn't get any better than that. Well, I suppose if you're JK Rowling it does, because she probably gets people saying this in their hundreds. OK, millions. But it really is the most fantastic feeling.

Changing someone's life even a tiny, weeny bit is quite a thing. Regardless of whether your book's won an award or not.

Which mine has, by the way.

Loanwords

2008

What do the following phrases have in common? *Objets trouvé. Haute cuisine. Hors d'oeuvres. À la carte. Au fait. Tète-â-tète. Bon appétit.* Well, yes, I know they're all in French. It's not just that. It's that they all have an easy English translation, and yet we opt to use the French. Why do we feel the need to say, '*au fait*' instead of '*familiar*'? I don't get it. It seems that with French idiom, as far as we Brits are concerned, *plus ça change, plus c'est la même chose.*

It's funny how so many of them tend to be food-based. We presumably like them because they sound a lot better in the language of a country that can cook, and isn't awash with American burger bars and microwaveable, processed TV dinners.

It's common knowledge that many English sayings, by contrast, tend to originate on ships (*batten down the hatches, give a wide berth, three sheets to the wind...*). Perhaps this simply reflects our historic national obsessions: the French with enjoying good food and drink, the Brits with getting on ships and enslaving as much of the world as possible. No, that can't be right – the French did a fair bit of that too.

But individual words are different. The English language is absolutely riddled with useful French words. Imagine a world without *menu, naïve, matinée, bistro...* and there are less obvious ones: *gauche, raconteur, voila, touché, rapprochement*. These are words for which we just haven't got round to inventing an English word. Or perhaps we did have one, but we couldn't be bothered to use it, and it got left behind to languish as 3-point type in the *Complete Oxford English Dictionary*, to be resurrected only if *Call My Bluff* ever makes a comeback.

Not that we're solely reliant on the French for these 'loanwords' (to use the proper, well, word). It's amazing how many of our everyday words have come directly from other cultures too. There are Hindi ones (*dinghy, chutney, pundit, pyjama, bungalow, jodhpur...*). And we'd never have *anorak* without the Eskimos. Of course when it comes to the most interesting loanwords you can always rely on those trusty Germans. They not only give us words for which we don't have an English equivalent, but they give us words that we didn't even know we needed! The incomparable *schadenfreude* (taking pleasure in others' misfortunes, or malicious joy) is a great example. Then there's *zeitgeist, angst, doppelganger, kitsch...*

You can guess what point I'm leading up to, what with this being a Cornish magazine an' all. Oh yes, Cornwall's got plenty to offer in the way of useful words too. I don't necessarily mean Cornish language words. It's the local slang words and idiom that are every bit as useful as these German and French ones. But as our county changes before our very eyes, we must act now if we are going to retain them. When my grandmother passed away it felt like we'd lost not only

245

Nan, but a significant cultural resource. You can make all the tape recordings you like, but it's not the same as chatting to an old Cornish person and a little gem suddenly popping out. But old Cornish people are disappearing fast. Globalisation is all very well, but I see a day looming when we wake up to find our culture has become relegated to demeaning T-shirts for the amusement of tourists with '*dreckly*' and '*proper 'ansum*' printed on them, like some sad novelty pastiche of something which was once real. Sorry if this sounds a bit paranoid, but I think it's true.

Plenty of our more generic words and phrases are still in everyday use (*scat down* for knocked-over, *chacks* for cheeks, *have a geek* for have a look...). Others are disappearing a lot more quickly (*smeechy* for smoky cooking smells, *clicky* for left handed, *fitty* for appropriate or proper).

A useful word or expression can easily be assimilated into everyday usage, especially if there's no obvious English alternative. This became apparent to me just the other day. Whilst on the phone to a friend upcountry (who's never lived in Cornwall in his life, poor chap), he told me that he hadn't been all that well lately, and was still feeling a bit *wish't*. Neglecting any concerns for his health, I immediately asked where he'd got the word. "Oh, I've been saying that all my life. I think it's a northern expression, isn't it?" was his reply. I can only assume that he'd heard my family saying it over the years (we can be a sickly lot, we Crosses), and adopted it without realising. There's no English word quite the same as *wish't*. Traditionally one should add '*...as a winnerd*' at the end, but

246

that's two old Cornish words in the same sentence, so let's not get carried away.

Of course there's the odd phrase that we should probably let go anyway, on account of the fact that they came from less politically correct times. Guess what the people of St Ives were referring to when describing a maid as 'Porthleven-built'. In Porthleven, apparently, they built boats with a wider rear end. I mean, stern. I mean *derrière*. Oh no, here we go again…

The thing
about spring

2005

S pring really is the best season, isn't it? You can keep your
monotonous grey months of mild mizzle that is our
Cornish winter, and the predictable disappointment of yet
another autumn that arrived all too soon, banishing any hope
of an Indian summer. In spring, everything's coming alive.
You've got it all to look forward to. Spring is wonderful.

Except for one thing. One thing that for me casts an
ominous shadow over this otherwise idyllic time. I refer,
regrettably, to a delicate subject: the disturbing antics of my
normally delightful geese. I'm sure that the same thing is going
on throughout the animal kingdom as the days get longer and
warmer, and all natural things succumb to the primal urges so
necessary in order to engage in the great circle of life. And I'm
sure that all birds go about things in a similar way to my
beloved pets. But when two twenty pound geese take it upon
themselves to express their love for each other five yards from
my conservatory, well, it downright puts you off your
breakfast. Especially when they're at it again ten minutes later.

If one happens to notice a couple of sparrows doing the
same thing, it doesn't seem so bad. You simply pretend not to

have noticed. It's quite sweet really, knowing that they'll soon be snuggling into their cosy nest and then introducing new little sparrows into the world. But with geese, well, there's water involved, splashing all over the place, and wings flailing, and the most alarming noise. And the violence! By the end of the breeding season the poor goose looks as if she's already half-plucked for Christmas, such is the tenacity of the gander as he grabs her by the neck with his huge orange beak in his frenzy to go the distance. Not since I watched that David Lynch retrospective on Channel 4 have I seen seen lovemaking so brutal.

The most unfortunate part of all this is that people tend to come and visit quite a lot in the springtime. And this being Cornwall, they want to sit outside and luxuriate in the rejuvinating sensation of warm spring sunshine on their skin. So you greet your guests, sit them in the garden amid mutual exclamations about what a beautiful county we live in, and aren't we lucky with the weather, and isn't Easter early this year, when guess what. Right on cue, the geese submit to their urges once more. Your guests' jaws drop. They simply don't know what to say. Or where to look. But you know what they're thinking. They're thinking, 'Good Lord! Are they really doing what I think they're doing? Is that normal? I mean, what can they possibly be trying to achieve!?' And, like the dog owner whose beloved pet attaches itself to their houseguest's leg the moment they step over the threshold, my wife and I fumble with some lame excuse. We've even tried joking about it: "Well, they're not called water 'fowl' for nothing!"

The cruel irony is that none of this business is necessary anyway, because as far as we can tell, our deviant gander is incapable of fathering children. His ladies start laying their enormous eggs towards the end of February (tradition states that Valentine's Day should herald the first goose egg of the season. Ah, sweet...). But no matter whether we let one of them go broody and sit, or bring some eggs in and try to incubate them on the Rayburn, nothing has yet emerged. Maybe it's our fault. Maybe we immasculated the gander when we named him 'Captain Beaky' on his arrival three years ago. Maybe if we'd named him Thor or Tiger he wouldn't have issues. But I'll say one thing for him, what he lacks in fertility he makes up for in enthusiasm. Maybe a little Viagra crumbled into his water would give the old boy a bit of a boost. Don't think I'm buying it for him though.

Thank goodness this sorry scenario doesn't last long. Geese aren't like hens, and have a much shorter laying season. After a few weeks, egg production begins to dwindle and everyone can reflect on what has passed. Clowance, the favoured female, by now looks half-dead. More pink and pimply than white and downy, she doesn't seem to notice, bless her. She's got another nine months to recover, grow some new feathers and brace herself for it all again next year. Poor Audrey, with her gammy leg (you may recall her accident from last year), lives life as a sexually frustrated spinster. Always the bridesmaid, never the bride. But it's not for want of trying. It's usually Audrey who makes all the noise as Captain Beaky and Clowance go about their dirty business. Presumably she's screaming something along the lines of, "What's she got that I haven't? Come on, don't let my trick knee put you off, I'm very bendy!" Or some such thing. But now she knows she's missed her chance for another year. As for the Captain himself, well, he looks as confused as ever.

Now that it's all over, my wife and I can again welcome guests to our garden whilst enjoying the company of these most endearing of feathered friends, and look forward to the best season of all.

Summer.

Jerusalem artichoke

2011

O ctober again. This time of year there's a vegetable that starts to show its ugly little face in our autumn veg box on a regular basis, and I have come to loathe it. It is truly the Gordon Ramsay of vegetables. It even looks a bit like him, come to think of it. Who in the world would, hand on heart, choose to eat the sad, wizened little monkey brains we call Jerusalem artichokes?

They belong to the genus *Helianthus*, and therefore, if left in the ground, would grow into a sunflower. That would be lovely. But no, we dig them up and pretend they taste nice. With mud lurking in every impossible-to-get-at crevice of their ludicrous form, you first have to spend twenty minutes scrubbing, peeling and de-knobbing the miserable little tubers. Then you've got to cook them. They are horrible roasted, and worse steamed or boiled. All the recipes you read about them basically involve disguising them with preferable ingredients. If you eat them mashed, they are apparently best mixed 50/50 with proper potatoes. Which rather begs the question, why not remove them altogether and use potatoes (a superior vegetable in every way, and available in huge sacks in laybys virtually all year round for a fiver)? And yes, I've tried grating them in a salad (as recommended in one of the missus' poncier vegetarian cookbooks), and I've tried Hugh Always-Eats-It-All's Cream of Jerusalem artichoke soup recipe. By the time I finished, I'd lost the will to live.

Oh, sure, everyone's got a magic recipe for dealing with the problem that is a Jerusalem artichoke. But I can't be bothered to listen to them anymore. These people are snobbish foodie types who reckon they've transcended the world of ordinary, popular vegetables. They are basically saying, "*If only you knew about this sort of thing like I do*". They are showing off. And they are fooling no-one with their, "*Oh yes, you simply must drizzle them with extra virgin truffle oil*". As far as I'm concerned the only thing to do with a Jerusalem artichoke (if you're not going to let it flower) is feed it to cattle. Which is apparently what sensible farmers in sensible countries do.

It's the same with nettles. I'm perfectly aware that you can make an acceptable soup with tender nettle shoots in spring. I've done it myself. And it's a comfort to know that when petrol hits £10 a gallon next year and no-one can afford to deliver food to shops, we can all make an acceptable meal from roadkill and objects found in the hedgerow. But I would never claim that a nettle, or a dandelion leaf (also technically edible but not very) is in any way comparable, let alone preferable, to a nice bit of, say, spinach.

Worst of all I get the feeling we're supposed to be grateful for the existence of Jerusalem artichokes, simply on the grounds that they're a bit unusual. "*Ooooh,*" you say at first, "*Jerusalem artichokes! A bit like a potato, and not related to an artichoke at all! How very novel!*" No! A Jerusalem artichoke is just a rubbish potato. A tuber that's really hard work, and tastes funny. Not to mention causing quite unacceptable levels of flatulence (or very acceptable, depending on your age).

Why revere such a vegetable? It brings nothing worthwhile to the table. It has nothing to contribute. Let's take a step back and look at ourselves, and stop this madness. I tell you, these foul vegetables are truly the Emperor's New Clothes.

No doubt there are Jerusalem artichoke-huggers reading this. But I make no apology. I have a feeling my comments may galvanise opinion in the same way they did when I wrote a few years ago about my distaste for opera (or, rather, my distaste for opera lovers arrogantly assuming that we would all adore opera if only we'd give it a chance). So, we'll see. Feel free to comment.

Ten years

2011

It's amazing to think that 2001 (that most futuristic sounding of years) was ten years ago. What a year that was, when you think about it. 2001 was the year Foot and Mouth disease took hold. There was 9/11. And it was the year someone thought it would be a good idea to open a vast greenhouse in an old claypit up Roche way (a greenhouse which went on to become our most famous tourist attraction).

But in case anybody's thinking that the opening of Eden was the most significant thing that happened around here in 2001, think again. 2001 was the year a completely natural event occurred which suddenly made Cornwall feel a lot more Cornish. The return of three very important black birds handed us our identity back, literally overnight.

The chough was, truly, Cornish again, and no longer the laughable oxymoron that it had become for most of my life. Those extinct birds which we were all taught about at school, the sacred bird of Cornwall, the legend, the soul of King Arthur, the very essence of everything Cornish, which had long been consigned to history books, pub signs and the distant memories of the very old, miraculously reappeared. It was fantastic. Those three choughs started living happily down on the Lizard cliffs, acting as if everything was perfectly normal, as if they'd never been away. That's typical of choughs, the cheeky devils.

I grew up in a Cornwall that had just the two choughs. They were a sad, lonely pair living up near Newquay, and they were officially the last two remaining in the whole of Cornwall. They'd both gone by 1973. And that was that.

Now, in 2011, we've had a legitimate, natural chough population for a whole ten years. Their numbers have slowly but steadily increased to the point where Cornish kids can take their presence for granted. Hopefully in the fullness of time, their 28-year absence will be considered a mere blip; a temporary inconvenience in the natural way of things.

And yet I know lots of Cornish people who haven't set eyes on one. Why is it that so many people still haven't bothered to go out and see our most important bird?

I can't guarantee that the sight of a Cornish chough flying over our cliffs will reduce you to a jibbering emotional wreck, but I did take Ern down to the Lizard to look for choughs last time he was back visiting from Australia. He's no birdwatcher, but he is a Cornishman. I didn't expect much of a response from him, and was fully aware that if a couple of large capacity motorcycles happened to go past at the same time as a chough, his eyes would probably be on the bikes. But we went anyway, and we had some really good views of the birds. It was almost as if they knew. And Ern was surprised. He loved them. He wasn't exactly rendered tearful and speechless, like I was the first time I saw them in 2001, but he was, for a time, visibly affected by seeing something he thought he'd never see.

During my many shifts down on the Lizard volunteering for the RSPB I've seen the phenomenon many times. A chough flying overhead and crying out often has a surprising effect on the observer. Give me the sight of a pair of choughs tumbling through a windy Cornish sky over a Royal Wedding, any day.

2011 is the tenth anniversary of the choughs' return to their ancestral homeland. You've had ten years. There's never been a better time to go out and see them. No more excuses. This is a call to arms. The Chough Project have even set up chough-themed events down on the Lizard in mid-June, so let's get out there.

It's not as if it's that hard these days. They're all over the place.

Fitting in III: Cars

2010

Welcome to the third in my occasional series designed to help the incomer to Cornwall assimilate into our Cornish ways. I've talked before about some of the best methods to fit in when you're new to Cornwall. Mostly it's been all about matters sartorial. So this month I think we'll take a look at cars.

If you're lucky enough to own a car, there are a few things you need to remember if you're going to look the part. To fit in down here you must drive an estate car, diesel, and at least ten years old. Ideally older. There should be some bale twine or tape holding something on. Obviously a local number plate helps, but bearing in mind that (since the scrappage scheme ended) not many people are interested in buying a new car, you can't always guarantee this. I've mentioned previously that *Kernow* bumper stickers were once used by locals who didn't have a Cornish number plate to declare their localness, but that their use has now become so commonplace as to render them meaningless. In fact these days a *Kernow* sticker is more often than not bought by holidaymakers, thus undoing all our good work.

Stickerwise, you're much better off with something a bit more specialised. *Pirate FM*, possibly, or the holy grail of

Cornish decal cred, an old *Lifeboats* sticker. A well-faded, original one, that's what you want. The dedicated incomer may have to resort to scouring breaker's yards to find a good original *Lifeboats* sticker (risking the incredulous gaze of the chap running the yard as he attempts to come up with a price for such an item). A sticker from your local surf shop is good, but again it must be very old and faded. *Surfers against Sewage* gets you instant credibility. A *Cornish Pirates* sticker is also good. It tells the world not only that you live here, but that you appreciate a proper local game played by Celtic nations, rather than any odd, spherical ball-based English versions in which players throw themselves to the ground and roll about screaming whenever a player from the other team comes near them.

You must never, *ever*, wash your car, as a filthy dirty car declares that you live somewhere so rural that you really don't see the point. Actually, there is no point. It's not as if cars are designed to ever be touched, and cars don't really rust any more, so it would be wasted effort. A Cornish car has to contend with a constant barrage of mud, drizzle, salt spray and goodness-knows what else. It will get filthy so quickly that if you clean it you're telling the world that you've got too much time on your hands. No, the only time you should wash your car is when the windscreen becomes so encrusted with gull guano that your wipers simply can't cope.

Ah yes, protocol for car security. We have friends who often come to stay from upcountry in an old banger that can't be worth more than £100. They park it in our drive and not only lock it, but apply one of those big clamps to the steering wheel. They do this even if their car is boxed in by other cars overnight. Now I don't want to encourage a Cornish crimewave, but this sort of vehicular paranoia just isn't that common down here.

There are plenty of other ideas for asserting your car's Cornishness. A towbar is a good idea. You don't ever have to tow anything. But a towbar declares to the world, 'I sometimes tow something. It could be a boat'.

You might want to leave things inside the car too, in case anyone looks inside for clues. A *West Briton* or *Cornishman* left carelessly on the passenger seat will also send out the right message, although there's a chance you could be a visitor looking to buy a second home. You wouldn't want that.

So, there you go. Follow these essential guidelines and you'll command instant respect. You'll never get a parking ticket, and people won't ever tailgate you, or overtake you on a dangerous bend, in Cornwall, ever again.

Yeah, right.